PRAISE FOR HYDRA IN WINTER

Reading *Hydra in Winter* is like drinking a bottomless glass of champagne—bubbly, refreshing, and bound to make you laugh.
 —Kyra Geddes, author of *The Story Thief*

I reckon if you write the way you eat cream buns, you're on a winner with *Hydra in Winter*.
 —the girl who works at the bakery

ABOUT THE AUTHOR

After a lifetime raising cattle on Queensland's Granite Belt, my husband and I traded bush life for the beaches of the Sunshine Coast. When I'm not writing novels, travelling and capturing my world through an iPhone lens, I'm marvelling at my clever grandchildren. I'm a member of the ALLWRiTE Club, a writers' group of memorable characters worthy of a novel on their own.

But my ultimate mission is the pursuit of the perfect cream bun.

My next novel *Son of Hydra* is set for release in 2025, followed by *Daughter of Cork* about the pirate's wife, and I have many more travel stories to come.

If you'd like to keep in touch—and perhaps join me on more adventures—I'd love you to subscribe to the readers' group on my website. The link 'waits you'—you'll understand that phrase after reading *Hydra in Winter*. -:)

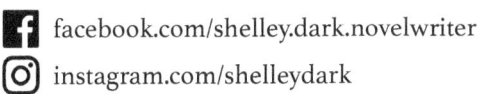

facebook.com/shelley.dark.novelwriter
instagram.com/shelleydark

HYDRA IN WINTER

AN ISLAND ESCAPE IN SEARCH OF A GREEK PIRATE

SHELLEY DARK

Copyright © 2024 by Shelley Dark

All rights reserved.

No part of this book may be reproduced in any form or by any electronic or mechanical means, including information storage and retrieval systems, without written permission from the author, except for the use of brief quotations in a book review.

Published by Shelley Dark Publications 2024

Cover image: Rony Dhar 2024

I DEDICATE THIS BOOK

to my husband John
for making every challenge lighter
and every success brighter

WITH MY DEEPEST THANKS

To the people of Hydra whose kindness shatters the historical myth of *'pride and insolence towards strangers'* (Pouqueville, 1822), but especially the staff at the archives, particularly Mrs Adamopoulou, Stam, Eleni and Panagiotis; and Maria Voulgaris, Katerina, Aileen, George; everyone who was so kind—thank you for the warmth of your welcome

To my fellow writers in the ALLWRITE CLUB, whose 24/7 friendship, support, and wisdom have seen me through crises both real and imagined—Kerry Anderson, Jude Anison, Kate Burns, Kerri Flanagan, Jenny Gibson, Natasha Granath, Michelle Harris, A'Mhara McKey, Catherine O'Neill, Brigita Ozolins, Kate Reynolds, Bri Weir, Leila Wright, Jo Mitchell, Jason Underwood, and Amy Barnett.

And to you, reading buddy—yes, you, with this book in your hands—thank you for the gift of your time, your trust, and your company

1

CHASING DAWN: BRISBANE TO ATHENS

I've left home.

Correction—*we've* left home buddies. And I'm thrilled you're coming with me.

The steady hum of the plane's engines reminds me of the miles passing below. As our aircraft inches across the in-flight map from Brisbane towards Dubai, my mind is racing as if I've downed five espressos. It's all I can do to stay in my seat. I'm a big believer in bloodlines, and if my husband's great-great-grandfather was a baddie, I need to know.

To calm myself, I take in my surroundings. I'm sitting next to Duncan, an Englishman straight out of a Jane Austen novel. Softly spoken, he introduces himself as a resident of the Côte d'Azur. Imagine that—lavender fields, palest rosé, the glare of white gravel... No, wait, that's Provence. Beaches crowded with sunburned bodies, rows of umbrellas, the glamorous chaos of Cannes...

I snap out of the daydream when he asks, "Where are you headed?"

I answer with a touch of smugness, "Greece. Actually, Hydra."

"Have you been there before?"

"No. This is my first time."

I've seen plenty of photos, and I know it's a car-free island with old mansions (*archontikó*) and enough naval history to sink a ship. It was a creative retreat in Leonard Cohen's time, when he bought a house on Hydra, and famously strolled around in sandals and mingled with Australian writers George Johnston and Charmian Clift. His muse, Marianne Ihlen, inspired him to compose '*Bird on a Wire*' there, and the island has also served as a backdrop for films like *Boy on a Dolphin*.

But I'm interested in its much older history.

Duncan's eyebrows lift. "Won't it be chilly?"

I nod, grinning. "Better than the heatwave at home. Besides, I'm on a mission."

Duncan smiles. "It's a long way to go to get cool."

I nod again. "My husband gave me a plane ticket for my seventieth birthday in December, and it's been burning a hole in my pocket ever since."

"What a gift! He didn't come with you?"

"No, he can't tear himself away from his surfboard."

He laughs. "Well, happy birthday! But why Hydra?"

"Thank you! I'm researching his family history."

As soon as the words leave my mouth, my brain whirs into overdrive. I know little about John's ancestor, but the scraps I have are driving me mad with curiosity. He was a young man during one of Greece's most turbulent eras—its War of Independence in the 1820s—and the thought of visiting his birthplace makes me giddy.

Back then, it wasn't a tourist destination—it was the nerve centre of Greek naval power. It's even possible he was the son of a wealthy shipowner—a position of great privilege on one of the three tiny islands bankrolling the naval war for a future Greece. Coming from such a powerful family would make the search for him easier. That's why I'm dying to get into Hydra's archives—they could hold the missing pieces of his story. With any luck, I'll finally put it all together.

"So your husband is Greek?"

"Partly. Although he didn't know it until recently." I might as well give him both barrels. "His great-great-grandfather was a convicted pirate."

Duncan's eyes widen. "A pirate? Wow."

"Well, he and his mates said they were freedom fighters, not pirates."

"So you're doing a family tree?"

"I may write a book about him."

Whoa. Where did that come from? My subconscious? Shouldn't we have had a team meeting first? Yes, I'm writing a diary for you, buddies. But a book? The altitude must be messing with my brain. Or was that a Freudian slip? I file it away to think about later. Maybe this wild idea has something to do with the little jewel of a book in my bag—*Travels with Epicurus* by Daniel Klein. I bought it because it's set on Hydra, and only coincidentally because Klein ponders the secret to authentic aging. It gets great reviews—the author studied philosophy at the Sorbonne as a youth, and he's read the great philosophers, so I trust his wisdom.

But I'm pretty sure I don't want to follow any advice on aging gracefully in the conventional sense—I'd rather channel my inner tornado. After all, life is, by definition, more about momentum than stillness, isn't it? Perhaps that's the reason I'm chasing a two-hundred-year-old pirate halfway around the world—taking a stand against the slow creep of predictability.

But why would I tell Duncan sitting there beside me in the plane that I might write a book?? That was absurdly ambitious. But common sense has never stopped me before.

The note of the aircraft's engines changes slightly and the muffled thud of the flight attendant's footsteps passing prompts my neighbour Duncan to ask another question.

"So," he says, "if you're writing a book about a pirate, Shelley, you must be a sailor?"

There's amusement in his eyes, as if he's testing me.

"Ah, that's a slight complication, Duncan. I've never been on a sailing ship. Their pirate ship was a schooner, and they attacked a brig. I thought a brig was a jail, and a schooner's a glass of beer."

Duncan laughs. "Not quite, but close."

Time to shift focus.

"So Duncan, what do you do?"

"I'm a ship's captain," he replies, smile broadening into a grin. "In the Mediterranean. Super yachts."

I scramble to wrap my head around this monumental coincidence. A ship's captain? In the Mediterranean? Really? Duncan launches into an enthusiastic explanation of the difference between a brig and a schooner. He knows the Mediterranean inside out—he knows every current, every weather pattern, and probably every fish by name.

We swap life stories and email addresses. Duncan shares what he's been doing in Australia, and I describe how my husband John and I retired from cattle raising and moved to the beach.

Duncan passes his tray to the steward.

I'm amazed that he ended up sitting beside me.

He's read my mind, because he says, "I wasn't supposed to be in this seat. I changed it yesterday, for no reason."

My jaw drops. "You're kidding. I did the same thing."

What are the chances of my sitting next to a Mediterranean yacht captain when I'm chasing a Mediterranean pirate—and both of us changing our seats at the last moment to make it happen? If this were a novel, people would say it was annoyingly unbelievable. But isn't that how the universe works? It hands you exactly what you need, right when you need it?

Suddenly, this trip feels less like a random adventure and more like part of some grand plan.

The lights in the aircraft dim and I try to sleep, but I'm still thinking about John's ancestor. *Ghikas Voulgaris*. The name is burned into my brain. Villain or hero. Patriot or man exploiting chaos for personal gain. Criminal or freedom-fighter. This isn't idle curiosity—he is family, after all—his blood runs through my husband's veins. And my children's.

He's the catchy tune I can't get out of my head—I have a burning curiosity about him and his family—also John's. His story is connected to mine too—and not just through my husband. Why else would I tell a stranger I'm writing a book about him?

Perhaps it was the excitement of the moment. Or perhaps I was showing off.

As we prepare for landing, I learn Duncan is heading to

Marseilles while you and I are off to Athens, buddies. We say our goodbyes at Dubai, and I continue my journey back in time, with dawn hot on our heels. As we descend into Athens, it catches up, and I'm enchanted by the way it touches the Acropolis with a blush of pink.

We touch down at 7am, and I suddenly realise—I'm about to disembark by myself.

But then I remember—you're with me. What a relief!

You can carry the bags.

Only joking.

You hail the taxi.

Seriously though, I couldn't be more excited to have you along. This trip is going to be special, and way more fun with you to share it.

2

ATHENS: BITTER ORANGES AND ANCIENT STONES

Athens, here we are! As we drive into the city at dawn, the first glimpse of the hillsides of Athens is magical. Soft grey shrubs drape the hillsides like a gauzy scarf, their ghostly leaves blending into the chalky white soil.

But in the city, what really catches the eye are the bitter orange trees (*citrus aurantium amara*) that line even the narrowest streets. These aren't just any trees—they're the supermodels of the botanical world, perfectly trimmed globes of deep green leaves, each one laden with hundreds of fluoro oranges. Imagine the perfume in spring!

I'm barely out of the taxi at the historic Hotel Grand Bretagne when I'm itching to explore. The grand dame's foyer comes with enough swagged curtaining to fit out a Broadway production of My Fair Lady and an ottoman the size of Hydra. During the wait for my room, I wander through the bar with its equally vast wall tapestry depicting the battle between the Greeks and the Persians, and then down to the basement pool. It's so James Bond, I half expect a motorboat to slice through the water with him at the wheel.

A quick shower, and I'm off to the CBD, dizzy with the thrill of finally experiencing Athens.

As I wander the city streets, the omnipresence of the Acropolis lures me on, every turn offering another jaw-dropping view of this dramatic cliff-edged plateau. It's like walking through a familiar movie set, where millennia collide in the most outrageous ways. Slick modern buildings stand guard over ancient sites, the divinely Byzantine next to Roman ruins. Gucci models strike poses next to Greek philosophers, deep holes reveal archaeological digs right in the middle of the city, rows of Roman columns are punctuated by potted ranuncula commas, and people wait in Krispy Kreme lines, making donut queues on exquisite mosaics. History everywhere, underfoot.

It's quite a shock to see the tiny 16th-century stone church of Agia Dynami—protector of pregnant women—sitting inside the soaring foyer of a 1950s building, which was once the Ministry of Education, and now a hotel. Underneath that lies a network of tunnels used to smuggle weapons during the War of Independence. And to cap it all off, another dig below revealed hints of an ancient altar to Hercules—the namesake of Ghikas' ship. Centuries of history, piled on top of each other like a chocolate layer cake.

This is a perfect example of how Athenians revere their historical relics—they walk over them, build around them, and weave them into everyday life. And there's not a skyscraper in sight to challenge the Acropolis. Clearly, the city has its priorities straight.

Athens: Bitter Oranges and Ancient Stones

Lost in the maze of Monastiraki, I ask a young girl for directions. Labrini, an absolute gem, insists on escorting me for half an hour, eagerly pointing out all the must-see spots. We part with a big double kiss and a hug. Tonight, as I try to spell her name, I learn it means 'bright' or 'radiant' in Greek. Labrini, you're a star!

Back at the hotel, wildly happy but dead on my feet, the real luxury isn't the room itself—it's the triumph of finding it after navigating the maze of sunflower-coloured hallways. Like many grand dames, she has her own personality—equal parts elegance and eccentricity.

As I settle myself and my laptop on the oversized hotel bed to edit the day's photos—a process I love—my thoughts shift to tomorrow's ferry ride to Hydra.

The island is only an hour and a half by hydrofoil, making it the summer playground of the Athens set, as well as the global glitterati. I've seen enough Greek travel brochures to imagine what it's like—the *ómorfi kósmos* (Greek for beautiful people) flocking in luxury yachts to the sparkling turquoise waters. Baking themselves to a crisp in the sun and diving like porpoises into the crystal sea. I picture them later hurling their white-linen-clad selves into waterfront bars to clink ice cubes in tall glasses.

Sounds terribly glamorous, doesn't it—but Ghikas wouldn't have had time for linen and lounging.

And hold your horses (or donkeys). This is winter. There's only a slow ferry tomorrow, and if I remember my geography lessons correctly, a Mediterranean climate means the island will be hibernating under a blanket of chilly drizzle or shivering in icy winds. We may not even see the sun. We'll need raincoats, not bikinis. And we'll be burrowing in the archives.

So instead of channelling my tanned Greek goddess, this Queensland girl has gone full-on arctic explorer—I've packed cashmere layers, a puffer jacket, and beanie and gloves to wander the maze of windswept streets in the gloom of short winter days. The only shoes I've brought, with a nod to frivolity, are a pair of glitzy sneakers to add a bit of glitter to the frostbite—I waterproofed them myself with what I hope was an effective spray. At night, I'm trusting the apartment's heating will keep hypothermia at bay.

I find my notes on Hydra's history, reminding me that Pouqueville, a French diplomat for Napoleon, wrote in 1820 that Hydriots were "the most courageous, as well as the most industrious, of all the islanders in the Archipelago." And Henry A. V. Post, an American naval officer and representative of the New York Greek Committee who sailed to Greece on a relief ship in 1827, distributing provisions and clothing to those affected by the war, described them as "the most finely formed and athletic men I have ever seen," and in the coffeehouses along the quay saw "the most uniformly well-dressed population to be found in any city in Europe"—so basically a 19th century equivalent of an Abercrombie & Fitch ad.

But my Ghikas isn't a fashion model. He's broad-shouldered, strong, and striking—a Greek warrior built for battle, not preening.

And Hydriots weren't all style and no substance. They were "distinguished by their pride and insolence towards strangers" and "notorious for their lawless and unruly dispositions," and "more ferocious and ungovernable... than the other inhabitants of Greece."

So they knew how to dress for dinner but weren't afraid to start a food fight.

During Post's brief stay in the city, he also remarked that "the streets were every night infested with drunken revellers, shouting, and singing, and firing their pistols".

I know a couple of descendants who inherited those rowdy traits. And when I read that, it makes me feel like I know Ghikas a little better, too.

I studied European history at school and university, but modern Greece was conspicuously absent from the curriculum. When I first learned about Ghikas, the only information I recalled about 19th century Greece was Lord Byron's involvement in a Greek war, the Ottoman Empire was crumbling, and Europe was cheering for the Greeks. After all, it was the Romantic era when people were swept up in admiration for the glories of Ancient Greece—the birthplace of philosophy, art, and democracy—who didn't long for its revival?

But to be fair, my knowledge of history was crumbling too when I was at university—too many late nights and not enough time with my textbooks.

I'm eager to meet the Hydriots—those proud, taciturn, secretive, ungovernable and occasionally ferocious people described by Pouqueville and Post. A bit like John after he's lost at croquet. Tomorrow we'll step back in time, to a place where everyone knows everyone else, where grudges and alliances between the powerful families may still be remembered today. The perfect setting for uncovering Ghikas' lineage. Provided I'm not dodging stray bullets.

Anyway, whatever happens, we'll chat to locals (those who speak English), visit the historic merchant mansions (the ones open in winter), eat Greek food (if any restaurants are open), explore the churches, monasteries, and perhaps cemeteries. And of course, soak up the *atmosfaira* and test out our few Greek phrases.

By the way, did you know Greeks don't call their country Greece? To them, it's Hellas (Elláda). Their language is Hellenic (Ellinikā), and they call themselves Hellenes (Ellines). But they're pretty relaxed about it.

That's enough trivia for today—and enough adventuring. After a satisfying session of photo editing, I close the laptop, pour myself a glass of wine, and step out into the darkness of the room's outdoor terrace.

I stop dead.

Night has fallen, and the Parthenon is brilliantly illuminated against the black suede of the night. Each marble column is bathed in golden light, highlighting both the architectural perfection and the centuries-old scars along the roofline where the stonework has crumbled. The entire structure glows, a luminous beacon rising above the dramatically shadowed cliffs below, their rugged lines accentuated by strategic lighting. At the base of it all, the magic carpet of city lights spreads across the plain.

In two millennia, this monument has seen the rise and fall of empires. It has watched as Greek tunics gave way to Roman togas, Ottoman robes, and traditional fustanellas. And tonight, my jeans and blazer—just one more costume in the endless line of observers.

Ghikas... it always circles back to him. He would have

worn the vraka, the black version of the fustanella, in one life, and western clothes in New South Wales in another.

Is telling his story becoming my new obsession? Obsession—such a loaded word, suggesting commitment, maybe even a career change. But I've already retired... haven't I? I always thought retirement meant slowing down, but I prefer the adrenalin rush of creation.

That's why Japanese philosophy appeals to me: a fulfilling life comes from the intersection of what you love, what you excel at, and what the world needs. In their view, older people still have a role to play, contributing to society in ways that matter.

Don't get me wrong. I admire people who find contentment in a quieter life, as I think Klein is suggesting—those who embrace a slower pace with grace. There's something beautiful about that kind of acceptance. I don't see myself finding it. Or even looking. I've always been more of a cork waiting to pop.

The thought of sitting at the kitchen table, forever sipping lukewarm tea, and discussing the weather, fills me with dread. And I'm not alone. Klein calls it the "epidemic of (old age) denial".

At the mere thought, confining straps tighten, holding me back. Let me out of here!

Maybe that's why Ghikas calls to me—such an intriguing man, a mystery waiting to be solved. And yet, few Australians seem to know anything about him—when they absolutely should. He was a pioneer, for goodness' sake—a Greek pioneer in a sea of convicts from the British Isles. Maybe that's why I blurted out on the plane that I'm writing about him. But the responsibility would be huge—what if I didn't do him justice? Fleeting thoughts, really, gone as quickly as they arrive.

From my vantage point, I also overlook the "old palace" on my left—the first royal palace of modern Greece, completed in 1834 after the war, now the parliament building. This is where you and I will watch the changing of the guard when we come back in a fortnight, to see those soldiers goose-stepping in the iconic pompom slippers.

Isn't travel the best? New places, fresh stories—so much to write home about! Except, of course, I'm not writing home. I'm writing for you.

I go back inside and get ready for bed. Before I drift off, I read a few more pages of *Travels with Epicurus*. Klein's thoughts on friendship catch my attention: he says we enjoy the company of friends because friends want nothing from each other.

What an absolutely perfect way to put it.

That's what makes having you along so special. I'm sharing this with you and expect absolutely nothing in return. After all, whoever you are—on the other side of the world, in a completely different time zone, or maybe even years from now—you're silent. And as the Epicureans say, "communal silence is the hallmark of true friendship".

I simply enjoy knowing you're there.

But enough navel-gazing—we need sleep!

Until tomorrow, buddies, when we set sail for Hydra.

3

WELCOME TO YDRA

My taxi driver to the port of Piraeus is called Evangelos—pronounced ee-van-zay-ohss. When I exclaim over the bitter orange trees again, he says, 'You will try not to eat them."

He's right. I will try. Not to.

He asks why I am going to Hydra—I take note he pronounces it EE-druh.

This time, I don't hesitate. I say I plan on doing some writing. Just to see how it sounds.

'You look like a writer,' he says.

Just as well I didn't tell him I was taking up welding.

Writing is creeping into everything—I'm thinking in words for everything I see. I've never considered writing an entire book before—the idea is both exhilarating and terrifying. I'd have to figure out who he was—sailor, ship's captain, shipowner's son with a rebellious streak—or make it up. Bringing the 1820s to life with historical accuracy is no small feat.

But first, I'd have to decide whether to write fiction or non-fiction. Perhaps fiction is the answer, filling in the gaps where history is silent—it's the "why" that interests me rather than the "who", "what", or "where".

But isn't making up the story instead of insisting on fact a bit like cheating?

Fiction allows freedom, but demands more of the writer—more imagination, more courage to take risks. Sticking to the facts is safer. But then again, safe is boring.

And boring is what I fear most—I have spent my life avoiding it.

But while I'm dithering about writing Ghikas' story, I'm scribbling this diary for you—a bit like saying you're on a diet when you're holding a cream bun. I'm wanting to entertain you—without committing to being a writer.

There's something thrilling about putting pen to paper (or fingers to keyboard) for this diary. Writing a book, though? I suspect it involves more than flinging words onto a page and hoping for the best—but really, how hard can it be?

Anyway, that's enough self-indulgent claptrap. We'll be too busy enjoying Hydra, and I'll be too busy capturing it, to overthink things like this.

At the Piraeus port, an old woman wanders among the waiting passengers, selling boxes of matches. Everyone pretends she isn't there. I feel a pang of sympathy—she is older than I am, and it's chilly in the wind. At least she isn't begging. I hand her a few euros and when she offers me a box of matches, I give her a smile and shake my head.

Without missing a beat, she puts on a theatrical show of

brushing away an imaginary tear and, with the flat of her hands together in a mock prayer, she gives a grateful pout.

But her eyes have already moved on.

Life can be brutally indifferent, can't it? Watching her, I realise any preoccupation with aging is trivial. While I contemplate Klein's ideas, she's out there in the trenches of survival, where every move is about scraping by, not pondering the meaning of life. It puts things in perspective.

The catamaran Flyingcat 6 is rather space-age looking, in white and two shades of lime green. The ride is glorious, with a brilliant blue sky and hardly a ripple on the water as we zoom across the Saronic Gulf between islands. The inhospitable hills rising out of the water show signs of rock terracing. Our ferry enters a narrow channel between the island of Poros (note: not Paros—that's a different island) and the mainland, where we stop briefly to let passengers off. As I gaze at the oh-so-Greek houses, I think of the apartment I've rented.

In my online searches, I thought we'd (you and I) stay right on the waterfront, and I stumbled upon the Hydrea Hotel—a shipowner's mansion built in 1803, sitting right at the western entrance to the port. Perfect. And the man who built it? Yes, you guessed it. A Voulgaris! He's the right age to be Ghikas' uncle.

I immediately had visions of channelling my inner shipowner—strolling the docks and inspecting my fleet.

Destiny, right?

Unfortunately, no.

Like most hotels on the island, it's "closed for the winter".

Undeterred, I turned to Airbnb.

I found a delightful, light-filled apartment with a tiny

terrace on the first floor, right above the water. It had to be near that hotel. Perfect for sipping ouzo at sunset, but was it available? Iliana, the contact person, quickly confirmed it was, and after a minor panic attack, I was about to press the BOOK NOW button. But might not that beautiful Voulgaris mansion/hotel make an exception for one quiet, very well-behaved guest?

So I went back to Google. To my surprise, I found another website listing the hotel, with the same contact name as the Airbnb: Iliana. Was this the same person? I sent her a message, and yes, her mother owns both the hotel (still firmly closed) and the apartment which was once part of it. Oh buddies, meant to be!

As we reverse away from the Poros dock, the propeller stirs the water into a pretty swirling jade.

In the strait between Hydra and the mainland, the wind and waves pick up and the water turns navy blue, but it takes only minutes to reach the calm of Hydra's harbour.

Calm that is, except for my heart, which is doing an Olympic sprint. The whitewashed houses hug the amphitheatre of hills around the sparkling water, much as they did in the 1795 watercolour I saw online, painted by Thomas Hope, now housed in the Benaki Museum in Athens.

It's difficult to imagine, but in the early 1800s, this sleepy harbour was one of the busiest in the Mediterranean. Throughout the 1700s they'd been building ships and trading and now they had an extensive fleet. During the Napoleonic Wars, the shipowners made a fortune by running Russian wheat through the English blockade of Europe—designed to starve Napoleon by cutting off his supplies.

Families like the Voulgaris grew so rich that rumours flew they were stashing gold on their roofs and hiding it in their water tanks. This was the heyday of the English navy, which led the rest of Europe to call Hydra "Little England".

Now, here I am, two hours by 'slow' ferry, about to step into another world—I'm alone, not knowing a soul, armed with only a handful of Greek phrases.

This is Ghikas' world, not mine.

Will I be an outsider, facing barriers I can't cross? What if I'm lonely?

I tell myself to snap out of it—fling those doubts overboard.

Focus on tomorrow. First stop, the Hydra Museum Archives—with over 18,000 documents, manuscripts, and books, hopefully I'll uncover more about Ghikas.

However, that brings up another stumbling block.

I don't speak or write Greek. I won't even be able to read the archive catalogue.

I wonder if they have any English resources or if I will have to navigate the maze of documents alone. Their email was down for a couple of weeks when I first started searching. I contacted Kelsey, a generous and helpful English expat who lives on Hydra and has a wonderful website called Hydra Direct—she helped me contact archive employees Stam and Nektarios. Stam initially agreed to help, but later said he couldn't. Perhaps they're worried I'm looking for an interpreter.

I'll sort that out when we arrive.

Unfortunately, Kelsey will be away when we're there.

As the ferry docks, I scan the quay, looking for someone holding a sign saying 'The White House' as

Iliana promised. No one. Not a soul glances my way. I'm invisible.

The only other person standing looking lost is a fashionably dressed young blonde in mirror sunglasses, talking on her phone. A tourist, surely. But I can't see anyone else remotely likely. I shift slightly to catch her attention and when she turns her head, I raise my eyebrows.

She holds her phone away from her ear and says, with a little impatience, "The White House? Shelley?"

I smile and nod as if I've won the lottery.

She extends her hand. "Manjola."

A donkey owner asks if I want to hire him, but my greeter has already grabbed one of my bags and made a break for it. She's bumping it along the quay over the uneven flagstones, polished by centuries of feet.

I hurry after her, only stopping to photograph the donkey. Near the point on the other side of the harbour, after a few shops that look closed for the season, we climb a few steps, revealing a wide view of the open sea.

The perfect vantage point to watch for approaching pirates!

I gasp at the sight of the white marble threshold—an immense slab stretching a metre outside the wide double blue doors. I'm admiring the pale blue window surrounds and the olive tree growing out of stone at the front door while Manjola unlocks them, then I'm amazed to see another metre of marble inside. The sheer scale is overwhelming.

But it's not just the marble.

This is a Voulgaris house—a real shipowner's mansion built over two hundred years ago by one of the most powerful families on Hydra. Standing here, I feel the weight of history—ships, wealth, war, ambition. And we're close to Ghikas already, early in the trip. Assuming, of course, it's the same family.

No sooner does Manjola put my bag down than she turns to go.

'Wait!' I say, head filled with a thousand unanswered questions.

I can't articulate a single one.

She hesitates.

'Um. What's the Wi-Fi password?'

She looks as if I've asked her to explain the meaning of the universe.

I follow her into the bedroom where she pulls open the heavy wooden shutters and light floods in. I open the windows to admire the view of the port as she picks up a small black router, turns it over in her hands and plops it back upside down on the desk.

To cut a very long story short, she makes a dozen phone calls and texts half of Greece. Eventually a man in Athens called Kostas tells me he will phone back in an hour with the password.

Manjola is obviously itching to get out of here, and I can't bear to keep her any longer. Too bad there is no manual for the apartment. Too bad about how to work the coffeemaker, or where to put the rubbish, or how the lights or air-conditioner work, or where to buy my groceries. I don't care. I'll manage. Adventure waits. Or lunch, at least.

As I wave goodbye to Manjola, it dawns on me—she's most likely a friend of Iliana, roped in to doing a favour. This wasn't her gig at all, but she's stepped in, bless her.

I look around the apartment.

It's all white (of course!), with high ceilings, white painted wooden floors, and minimal touches of grey on the doors and the huge solid wooden shutters. The plastered stone walls are 600 millimetres thick—that's two feet! Imagine the events they have witnessed—and they'll continue to bear witness for centuries to come.

It makes me think of the eldest Voulgaris brother, Giorgios—another of Ghikas' uncles?—who twice saved the Turkish Grand Admiral's life and, in 1802, was appointed governor of Hydra by the Sultan himself.

The lavish Ottoman-style mansion the Turkish admiral gave him was a symbol of the affection in which he was held. His appointment, however, was a strategic move, meant to stabilise the island after civil unrest—including the assassination of a shipowner's father at his son's wedding.

As governor, Giorgios became the undisputed leader of the island, mediating disputes between shipowners and sailors over taxes and profit-sharing. With the backing of some of the important families, he kept the pro-Russian faction in check, bringing a measure of calm to Hydra's volatile politics.

Talking about calm, I didn't eat any breakfast this morning, in case I was seasick.

By this time, I'm so starving I could eat a bitter orange.

Kostas told me to eat lunch at Psarapoula. I climb steep white stone steps from the port, reading on a sign on the way up that the restaurant has been open since 1911, and then up a steeper wooden stairway to a rooftop restaurant with a splendid view of the town. The other diners are eating inside, out of the wind.

The waiter understands my order (impressive, because I'm not entirely sure what I've ordered myself) and the pasta with shrimp that arrives is an utter delight.

Next on the list, in order of importance, are flowers.

Nothing says I'm a writer faster than a vase on the desk. When I finally find Seaside Rose in the maze of spotlessly swept streets, I'm greeted by—wait for it—a Voulgaris! They're everywhere. And her name is Katerina. We chat about her stock, and I buy pink alstroemeria.

But flowers aren't enough. I need something sweet.

I follow the tantalising smell coming from an oven to an almond shop. I buy six wafer-thin slabs of golden brown flaked almond crunch.

After one bite, I understand why they've been in business since 1930. It reminds me I've read there's an almond blossom festival here in February. I hope we see it.

On my way home, I find a house in the backstreets that I'm sure has my name on it. Hydra is the prettiest little town, and when I finally carry my flowers up my front steps, it's like stepping into a postcard.

As I head out again to buy groceries, I call in at the nearby shops. I meet red-headed Sophia who introduces herself and tells me to call in any time with any questions I might have. Then there's George, who's travelled all over the world and lives upstairs. Spiros designs jewellery inspired by the octopus, and stocks Byzantine-style multi-coloured pieces with semi-precious stones, made by his best friend.

"Two fifty euro," he says, "but for you, one fifty."

Everyone is having a sale. There aren't a lot of customers at this time of year. And everyone has a cousin or a friend who lives in Australia. A small world, and a chatty one.

As I wander the town, I marvel at how tiny it is.

The island is long and narrow, with a steep, mountainous spine—rocky, barren, and with hardly any fresh water. It has to be shipped in or desalinated at Mandraki a couple of kilometres from the port.

Today, around two thousand people live here, but at its peak, Hydra housed over 20,000—wealthy shipowners, ships captains, and sailors. Everyone had a stake in the island's booming economy. I can't imagine where they fitted.

I enter the grocery store.

Pete sits behind the counter at the front door, calling out constant instructions in Greek that sound like 'get this', 'fetch that'. I ask if I can drink the water.

Pete answers in English. 'Yes, you can, it's not dangerous. But it doesn't taste good. Everyone buys water. Where are you staying? I'll deliver it for free.'

Before I know it, I've bought enough water to fill a swimming pool, some still, some sparkling. I sort out the cow's milk from the goat's milk, taste-test and buy some local cheese. There's not much in the way of fresh fruit. I climb upstairs to search for tinned peaches and crackers and stumble upon a jar of green olive paste made in Greece. A pear, an avocado, a big ripe tomato, and an apple, and I am done.

Pete has it all delivered by a man and his small son before I've finished paying. When I walk out of the shop, I can see them waving at me from my front door.

Greek hospitality at its finest.

Just when I think I've met everyone, along comes Skotádi —well, that's what I'm calling him. It means 'darkness' in Greek, fitting for a sleek, fat black cat who follows me to my door, winding around my legs and purring his way into my heart.

When I sit on my little terrace overlooking the harbour, I scratch his ears, and we are both exactly where we're meant to be.

He looks up at me with piercing eyes, almost as if he's speaking.

In ancient Greek plays, a group of performers were called the Greek Chorus—it was their job to comment on the action or the performance, offering wisdom or warnings.

For a moment, I think Skotádi is channelling the Chorus. Or is that the wind whispering?

"Will you rush off, or will you slow down for once?"

Later, at sunset, after I've unpacked my bags, the lights around the port reflect in the water.

A few people wander along the quays. The donkeys that stood around the water's edge all day waiting for carting jobs are gone. I imagine them unsaddled, brushed, fed full of hay, and put to bed.

I write a few paragraphs as if I'm starting a novel, and nod with approval.

I could be the next Hemingway, or Charmian Clift—or is that the wine talking?

As I replay the day's events in my mind, I think of home. Australia is just waking up. Our kids, our grandchildren. John will be stirring, looking at the surf report. He's taken to retirement with the same obsessive energy he poured into raising cattle—into growing pastures, animal genetics. Now it's photography, surfing, croquet, lawn bowls—he's making up for lost time. He leaves the house at dawn and comes home only to eat dinner and fall into bed.

We're alike in that way, never able to do things halfway. Yes, I've swapped my quasi-Versailles country garden and secateurs for an iPhone. And I've dived into Instagram, combining my own love of photography with my interest in anything tech. Each day, I post sunrise photos from my beach walks and I've gathered a small Insta-crew to 'walk' with me. Playing bridge is a three-times-a-week humiliation, and I drag John on international trips—when he agrees to come. I've written and sold my travel diaries. But none of these new activities have seen me leaping out of bed in the dead of night to scribble notes as I used to, or—more critically—made me forget to eat.

Maybe one day, something will pull me in with the same intensity again. I'm hopeful... but not holding my breath. And yet, here on Hydra, I feel charged up with purpose, as if I've stumbled into an epic story starring, well, me. It's an absolute delight, and I am not remotely alone. The idea of writing a book can wait—tomorrow is all about soaking up the magic of Hydra. Rain (so the forecast says) or shine, we're off to the archives, you and I.

It's 9pm and pitch dark outside. As I close the shutters, the moored boats outside my window rock at their moorings, the water slapping the stone edge.

A novel lullaby.

I take a hot shower and hop into bed with Klein's book. I love the bit about the ancient Greek concept of time: chrónos is the measured, ticking seconds of daily life, while kairós represents those rare, significant moments that transcend ordinary time.

Hydra is kairós.

As *koimithoúme, fíli*. Let's sleep, friends.

4

SECRETS OF THE ARCHIVES

At 7am, my mind is on the archives and the need to fuel up for day ahead.

I recall Kostas' tip to visit the bakery near the Piraeus Bank, but I'm wondering if my supposedly waterproof shoes will survive the downpour outside. The promise of fresh, warm bread draws me into the rain, like a sailor enticed by the sirens' irresistible call—those mythical Greek voices that led many to their doom. And if they were lucky, past a bakery.

The sea is flattened to a millpond—unrecognisable from yesterday's chop.

The wet flagstones are as slippery as an ice rink. I pick my way carefully around the harbour like a cautious penguin.

Streams of water gush across the quay in my path, as the higher streets empty into the port. Miraculously, my shoes hold, and I avoid doing a water slide.

Bags of rubbish lie against house walls, waiting for

collection by the teeny rubbish truck—one of only two vehicles on the island. Cats have torn a few bags apart, scattering the contents. One cat is snoozing peacefully in the rain, living its best life without a care in the world.

I find the bakery up a side alley. My stomach feels hollow when I see the empty shelves. Surely not closed for the off-season.

"*Kaliméra,*" I say. "Do you have bread this morning?"

"Yes, half a kilo or a kilo?" the smiling owner asks.

What a novel concept to buy bread by weight. I opt for the safer sounding half kilo, and right on cue, the baker emerges from the back with a tray of steaming loaves, which he tips onto the counter with a satisfying clatter.

Sheltering under my umbrella on the way home, I cradle the warm bread against my chest. Bread has never smelled as good! The crust cracks under the knife as I cut a thick slice. I cover it with scrapes of cold butter and eat fast before it melts.

I close my eyes.

For the second jagged slice, I drizzle golden Greek honey over the butter and let it soak in. Now my hunger has eased, I take my time eating, the sticky, buttery mess oozing over my fingers.

I lick it off. How can something so simple taste so divine?

I'd like to stuff in another slice, but I'm too full.

Keats wrote sonnets about ordinary things, didn't he, like "Ode to a Grecian Urn"? He found the extraordinary in the everyday. And Shakespeare did too.

I start…

Thou crusty sentinel of the Greek breakfast table, thou bearer of solid butter and honey…

An occasional heavy shower thuds against the window as I sit at the computer. Let's hope it eases before we go to the archives. They're beckoning from across the water.

We're amateur sleuths on the brink of a big discovery.

But before I get too carried away, I make a list of what I know about Ghikas to help at the archives:

1. **Name:** Ghikas Nicholaos Voulgaris, born Hydra somewhere between 1807-1809.

2. **Act of Piracy:** Nine men, including Ghikas, robbed the *Alceste*, a Maltese ship, south of Crete in July 1827. They hurt no one—a relief—but only nine men—how did they overpower an entire ship?

3. **Their pirate ship:** The *Herakles*

4. **Crew:** Captain Andonis Manolis, plus seven others including Ghikas (I have their names, ages and appearance from the register of their arrival in New South Wales).

5. **Arrest:** A few days after the act of piracy, the nine men were arrested by the English off the coast of Africa with stolen goods on board.

6. **Trial and Sentence:** The following year, seven were convicted of piracy and sentenced to death by a British court in Malta.

7. **Sentence commuted to transportation:** Seven were transported to Australia in 1829.

8. **Pardon:** In 1836, the English government granted them an absolute pardon and offered them free repatriation to Greece.

9. **Refusal of repatriation:** Ghikas Voulgaris and Andonis Manolis elected to remain in Australia. The other five accepted the offer.

The story, of course, is much bigger than that.

Most of what I know comes from Hugh Gilchrist's *Greek Australians, Volume One*, published in 1992—a proper tome—drop it, and you'd break a toe. Gilchrist, a former Australian ambassador to Greece and lover of all things Greek, devoted three full chapters to these Greek convicts.

He thought that Ghikas might be the son of a rich ship owner, because his death certificate at age 74 showed his father as "Nicholaos, *gentleman* of Hydra", mother's name "unknown".

Gilchrist, who died in 2010, believed that *gentleman* was code for shipowner, speculating that Ghikas was likely the son of one of the six brothers in the wealthy Voulgaris ship-owning family at that time. And I have a hunch he was right. I wish Gilchrist were alive so I could speak to him—he must have done a great deal of research.

But he also wondered, if that were true, why was Ghikas' name missing from family records?

So you can see it's complicated. And to further understand Ghikas and his motives, I need to understand the era he lived in.

He was between twelve and fourteen when the War of Independence against the Turks broke out in 1821.

By 1827, Hydra had turned into a full-blown soap opera.

The ship-owning families—Ghikas' likely among them—had funded the war with their money and their own ships, and they were squabbling with each other over their losses and turning to piracy to recoup them. They were also at the throats of mainland factions about how to run the new country, if there ever was one.

Meanwhile, at home, the unemployed sailors were

rioting in the streets over back pay (or no pay), and they were turning to piracy too.

People were starving, and pinning their hopes on English, French, and Russian intervention.

Even parts of Greece were English—the Ionian Islands had been snatched up after the Napoleonic Wars. The colonial appetite, even close to home, was insatiable.

Yet given that Ghikas and his mates were convicted of piracy and sentenced to death, it's a bit of a mystery why the British spared their lives. Gilchrist said it was because the trial procedure was suspect, but political pressure could have had something to do with it.

And another thing. Why did Ghikas choose to stay in Australia when they were pardoned, rather than return to Greece? Was there nothing left for him at home? Had he been disowned?

Hopefully, today we'll find out. The archives wait.

ARMED WITH THIS SKETCHY INFORMATION, I walk over, thrilled to finally meet Stam (Stamatis Kalafatis), the employee I've been pestering by email about my research.

He greets me with a warm smile from behind the front desk and introduces me to his charming boss, Mrs. Adamopoulou. Then I meet the archive manager, Eleni (El-ay-nee) Mavroudhkou, and Panagiotis (Pah-nah-yoh-tees) Amarianos, a friend of the archive.

All seem eager to help me. I'm relieved.

I explain what I'm looking for.

They nod knowingly—they've heard of these Australian

renegades, but from what I gather, that's about as far as their knowledge goes.

I ask if they have the book about the Voulgaris family, written by a Papamanolis in 1930—Gilchrist mentioned it, only to say that Ghikas wasn't in it. But you never know. I'm not sure what they say.

I'm shown to the archive library room on the second floor, where I sit at a massive table across from Eleni and Panagiotis. They speak rapid-fire Greek, turning pages, lobbing occasional questions my way.

As I do my best to keep up, my mind drifts back to that night in the '90s at our farm dinner table when our son dropped the Greek bombshell that started all this.

"Dad," he began, "you know how Nana was born down on the Monaro?"

Monaro, for the uninitiated, is a high treeless plain near the Snowy Mountains in Australia, a few hours south of Sydney. Nana was his grandmother.

John nodded, fork in mid-air, and Ben continued, "Well, are we Greek?"

John and I exchanged confused looks, but Ben continued, "We were doing a story down on Monaro last week, and someone told me I'm descended from the first Greek convict in Australia. Through Nana. He came from Hydra, and he was a pirate."

John's mother had more English sang-froid than a cup of Earl Grey tea. Curious, I leaned forward.

"Who said that?" I asked, already seeing parrots and eye patches.

Ben shrugged, slid a piece of paper across the table, and

asked, "Do you think it's true?" Neatly written in pencil was the name: *Ghikas Voulgaris*.

In that second, I was hooked. My mind was doing cartwheels—no, more like a full-blown circus routine—a pirate ancestor? Arrr!

John, more focused on his steak, muttered something about it being a joke. But I already had the Jacaranda atlas out, tracing the Greek coast until I found Hydra. Or more correctly, Ydra. My brain did more gymnastics.

Other people have exciting ancestors, not us. I was as delighted as if it were my own family.

"If you want to know more, Mum, you do it," Ben said, brushing off my idea that he go on the TV show Who Do You Think You Are.

So here I am, sitting in the archives, on Hydra.

Eleni's English is good, Panagiotis' so-so, but together they make excellent detectives.

As I stare at the endless rows of musty books and faded documents, I'm hit by a pang of overwhelm.

How can I piece together the fragmented history of a pirate from centuries ago when I don't even speak the lingo? Giving up isn't an option, but it's looking more and more like finding an olive pip in an ocean.

At one point, Panagiotis says, "You are kind. You have a special energy."

I'm glad because I have given them an enormous job. And they don't appear to mind at all.

Voulgaris is a common name, yet they can't find any mention of Ghikas. They search for the names of his fellow convicts. No result. And I can't understand what they are saying to each other, so I can't make suggestions.

This is looking like a debacle.

However, Eleni says the record-keeping about the island's ships was immaculate.

She finds one ship named the *Herakles* built in 1816—she will have the details next time I visit. What an exciting development! Research is supposed to be straightforward, isn't it? You find the facts, you piece them together, and *ópa*—a story emerges. That's the easy version.

Meanwhile, I am increasingly fascinated by Panagiotis' glasses. The arms are thick cast silver, shaped like sinuous branches. I ask where he bought them.

"I designed them," he says.

A silversmith too! Is there anything this man can't do?

"You should work for Bulgari!" I exclaim, struck by a sudden thought. Often in old records, Ghikas' last name was recorded as "Bulgaries" or "Bulgari". Could the name of the famous jewellery house Bulgari be an Italian form of Voulgaris? Later, I do some digging and discover that the founder of Bulgari was a Greek silversmith named Sotiros Voulgaris!

The different spellings are all variations of the original Greek name. The Greek letter Beta was pronounced as "B" back then. These days, it's pronounced as a "V". Hence the mix-up!

He laughs loudly. "You know they're not silver, don't you?"

I shake my head, completely fooled.

"Well, they're not!" He laughs again, delightedly. "I made them with sticky tape! I wound silver paper around and around, and then taped over the top!"

I am as tickled as he is. Eleni is smiling affectionately.

My new friends. Their eagerness to help makes me think

Secrets of the Archives

I've found co-conspirators in this little adventure. It's heartening to know I'm not alone in my quest.

While all this is happening, a man in a black cassock comes into the room and takes a seat on my side of the table. After a brief hello, the others ignore him, which seems strange for a man of the cloth.

I extend my hand. "I'm Shelley."

"I'm George," he says, with a warm handshake.

George contributes to the search and discussion. He gets up and rummages through cupboards. Panagiotis is at the end of a row of library shelves, rifling through books. Now and then, when Panagiotis calls out, Eleni rolls her eyes at me, smiling.

George seems interested in history, so I ask him about the War of Independence.

That's all it takes.

His English is excellent, and he's off on a monologue about the Turks, the Muslims, the Ottomans, the Romans, the Byzantine (there is NO such thing and anyone who uses the term is a criminal!), the divided Greeks, the Jews, the Egyptians, Hydra, its rioting sailors, dreadful massacres. People didn't value human life the way it's valued now. The lines between heroism and criminality were blurred.

"Things were fluid," he says. "It's hard to make categorical statements."

I think he just did.

Exhausted from his epic monologue, he sits again.

"Are you a priest, George?" I ask, feeling a little disrespectful.

"Yes," he says. "I'm doing a thesis on a religious topic at

about the same time in history as you're interested in. I come here to do research."

"May I come to see your church?" I ask. That feels odd too. I'm making it sound like a tourist destination.

"I'd be delighted," he says, and writes his name and the name of his church.

Despite all the effort, we seem to have come to a dead end. Eleni gives me the photocopies; Panagiotis begins packing up.

"So that's it?" I ask, my enthusiasm deflating like a punctured balloon. "There's nothing more I can do?"

Eleni hasn't found the Papamanolis book. I remind myself that research is about perseverance. It's a treasure hunt, and sometimes you must dig through a lot of sand to find the gold.

They confer briefly, and then George, ever the optimist, offers a suggestion. "Go to the cathedral. Enter the door under the clock tower. Go inside and ask to be taken to the gallery. Then ask for the services of the municipality. You may find something there."

Good old George. Although I'm not quite sure where he means.

I take a photo of Eleni and Panagiotis. When I look at it later, they have such kind eyes. And one of George too.

I thank them all profusely, promising to return—no, I'm not finished yet, but gently, gently—and I wander into the museum proper. Exquisite swords and silver-tooled pistols, Hydriot clothing, old documents, jewellery, and paintings. Even their much-loved Admiral Miaulis' heart in a container.

Secrets of the Archives

Back downstairs in the shop, I buy a book about the museum's treasures and a CD.

With photography banned, the only way to take the memories home is to buy them—an understandable way for a small, probably under-funded museum to boost its finances.

As I leave, Stam at the front desk suggests that when I finish my book, I should launch it at the museum. A lovely idea, Stam. I love how you can call yourself a writer, and people believe you. Then again if you say you're a plumber, they believe that too.

I'll earn the title one day. Writer that is.

A finished novel and a book launch on Hydra—the thought is surreal! Imagine having a launch party right here, with people gathered around, discussing my words and my thoughts. It's an out-of-body experience thinking about it.

But what if they said I hadn't captured Hydra or Ghikas' life as they deserved? The thought sends a chill down my spine. But wouldn't meeting the challenge of finding words that truly honour this place and its history—words that would have the locals nodding in approval—wouldn't that be the thrilling part?

It makes me feel slightly queasy.

Oh, for goodness' sake. It. Don't let it turn you into a nervous wreck. Get over yourself.

Outside, the weather has fully cleared. The canvas of sky, mainland, and sea is a study in blue: azure, pastel, and sapphire, each band separated by the finest pencil line. Panagiotis catches up to me a little way from the archives as I photograph a group of cats, two sitting nonchalantly on an old cannon and another standing up with his paws on the back of the park bench. Excitedly, he points out the building next door—the naval academy. It's been turning out ships' captains since 1749, mainly in the early days with Portuguese and Italian lecturers. Isn't that something?

We say goodbye again, and I head around to the cathedral.

It's locked—I'll give it a shot another day. Everything in its own time.

What's this? Don't tell me I'm settling into Hydra's tempo!

A creature of habit, I return to Psarapoula for a very late lunch of the most delicious mushroom risotto with truffle oil. With a side of steamed green spinach to make me as strong as Popeye. When I've almost licked the plate clean, Ilias, who works there (or owns it?), approaches me. I think he asks if I want the bill because they want to go home.

So I say yes.

But he is offering complimentary fruit—apple and orange, roughly peeled like your mother used to—not like a fancy restaurant. It is surprisingly comforting.

I'm careful about descending the wooden staircase before the stone steps. Note to self: avoid too much wine at Psarapoula.

Back on the quay, I say "see you later" to a lone donkey, her forehead marked with a disc to ward off the evil eye. I make my way home, and even though my time at the archives didn't yield much, it's been a wonderfully happy day, hasn't it? It wasn't about finding answers, though there's a chance I did. It was about the warmth of people like Eleni, Panagiotis, and George, who made me feel welcome and part of their world.

Secrets of the Archives

Even when things didn't go as planned, there was a shared sense of camaraderie and adventure.

I've just read what I wrote last night, and my inner critic pointed out all the flaws.

I told her to be quiet. Politely.

Then I read a little more of our friend, Klein, who talks about life on Hydra being *andante*—a musical term I haven't heard before.

It means to play at a walking pace, a gentle, unhurried rhythm.

On Hydra, because of the no cars and steep steps, *andante* is a way of life.

This is why I'm noticing details more—the curve of a donkey's ear, the texture of the stone underfoot, the clack of the boats rocking at their moorings. All my senses are heightened.

Heightened anticipation for bed too.

Until tomorrow, buddies. Not sure what the plan is. A little exploring? Let me surprise you.

Maybe I'll write a little more till bedtime.

Kalinίkta, filarákia, apó tin Ídra.

It's night-night buddies, from Hydra....

5

LOITERING ON HYDRA

Forget exploring. Today, we're embracing the art of *andante*.

We're loitering.

Exploring sounds too much like hard work—as if there's a destination or goal in mind. Loitering is the opposite. It's about wandering aimlessly, letting the day unravel however it wants. It's a bit of an art form. There are rules—unspoken, of course. Rule number one: don't have a plan. The second you make a plan, you're not loitering, you're wandering, and that's a different beast entirely. Rule number two: be prepared to go nowhere fast. Progress is the enemy of loitering. And finally, rule number three: let the world come to you. Sometimes, the best things happen when you're standing still, doing absolutely nothing.

Charmian Clift described our ideal day in *Peel Me a Lotus* —one of those "slow, golden afternoons where the light hangs perfectly, time pauses, and there's nowhere else to be and nothing else to do."

But first, we must deal with the weather.

You know those winds that make you look down, even though you know your jacket's zipped up? The ones that make you double-check you're wearing your scarf, and wonder why you left your beanie at home? Well, we have one today. But not all day. This morning it rains, after lunch it is plain miserable, and late this afternoon it is icy-windy-sunny.

Today, the "grand plans" George Johnston wrote about in *My Brother Jack* are officially *out*. As he put it, "life's in the unguarded moments, those accidental spaces between grand schemes."

"It's the small moments, the unguarded ones, that give life its true meaning. It's what happens in between the great plans."

We are in a moment *between* them.

But to add a *teeny tiny* bit of structure to this day of intentional aimlessness, I make a list of things to do and places to find. *Faux loitering*, you could call it.

But Hydra doesn't make it easy to find anything. It's like a gorgeous, lazy cat that stretches out and says, "Yes, I'm fabulous. Figure it out yourself."

But nothing can dampen our enthusiasm, buddies; Hydra has us under its spell.

So that's our plan for today—no *great* plans at all.

I find a tourist map hidden in a booklet on a shelf—don't you love a good booklet? The centrefold map inside would be extremely helpful if you were trying to find every hotel in town (when you already have your accommodation). But try to find Kala Pigadia? —the site of some wells which Ghikas' Uncle George had installed in the early 1800s? Good luck

Loitering on Hydra

with that. But I spot something else, rather intriguing, on the map: "Spoiled Shop." I wonder if it was once "Really Fresh Shop" before things went downhill.

My phone pings with a notification from ViaMichelin to check the holiday traffic. Outside the window, I can see eighty-two parked boats and one man with a box on a trolley. Thank goodness for ViaMichelin, or I might have missed him.

Armed with my half-useless map and an even more useless ViaMichelin app, we'll set out and let the island guide us.

Yesterday's shuttered shops have sprung open today—thanks to the tourist boat providing Hydra's version of rush hour—twenty people.

I watch two local women use a 'pulley' system to haul groceries up to a balcony, bypassing the hundred steps they'd otherwise have to climb. A pulley system and a bit of ingenuity beats modern technology!

I recognise a few faces from yesterday, and they give me a smile and a nod. I like that.

In a dress shop aptly named "Hydra", I meet Vaso and Katerina.

I ask if they can think of anyone to give me a historical tour—someone who knows about Hydra's revolutionary past. They don't know where Kala Pigadia is either (or maybe it's my accent?), but Katerina suggests a local history teacher. I hand over my details and cross my fingers. Their willingness to help gives me a lift. I might be another clueless tourist, but I'm starting to realise I can hold my own when it comes to chatting about the island's past. All that reading at home is paying off.

I drift toward the church and cloister. The bell tower—*kampanarió* in Greek—feels understated, a lot like Hydra itself. A large piece of marble with a two-headed eagle sits on the wall—a striking emblem.

The cathedral, as the locals call it, is smaller than I expected, its interior solemn and hushed. Sunlight filters through the narrow stained-glass windows while flickering candles cast a soft glow on the ornate beaten silver- and gold-clad icons. The entire altar backdrop is carved from marble, a masterpiece of intricate detail. The atmosphere compels silence.

George must have meant the gallery in the cloister. I climb the steps, wandering through one overheated room after another, until I find a tired-looking administrator with kind eyes snuggled up to a computer.

She barely raises her hand to the keyboard before she pauses and drops it again, as if the Herculean effort required is too much. She smiles apologetically, clearly wishing she could help. We're both devastated how her energy has drained away.

The lively girl running the Ecclesiastical Museum is eager to assist, and it energises me again.

I smile when she suggests, "Why don't you try the archives?"

Little does she know, it was George at the archives who sent me here in the first place.

Still, I enjoy roaming her three rooms filled with treasures—jewelled hats, exquisite silver and gold religious objects, vestments, old books.

She hands me her phone number. "Call me for anything," she says with a smile.

Loitering on Hydra

"Do you know where Saint Constantine's church is?" I ask. "The one on the block of land where his family home was, where he lived as a child?"

Uh oh, I think I just started loitering with intent.

She walks along the verandah and points way up the steep hill behind the town. I mentally note it for a future warrior-woman day. Saved.

For lunch, I wander into Miato—or so I think. Turns out it's actually Piato, which explains the plates covering the walls and ledges. Greek letters are confusing, but the broccoli soup is divine, and the wine is perfectly chilled. Any idea of heading back to the archives fades away—let's loiter a bit longer. I'm turning Greek—don't be surprised if I start shouting "opa!" and smashing plates. But not the plates on the walls.

Outside, I start taking photos—first one doorknob, then another.

Soon, I'm on a mission to capture every door and doorknob in the back streets behind the port. The pharmacy, which has been in business since 1890, is closed. Siesta, perhaps. Or the… yes, the off-season. Either way, I'll be back.

I climb to a round church dome and beyond, my Apple Watch nearly bursting as it logs 30 flights of stairs. It's underestimating, of course, but at least I'm not cold any longer. I finally stumble upon Kala Pigadia and the wells. The expat houses, Cohen et al, are somewhere around here, but I'm not driven to find them.

On my way back, I pass the mustard-coloured Kountouriotis mansion on the hill, usually open to the public, but not today—it's the… off-season.

Rumour has it that Lazaros the owner, the richest man

on Hydra, lost an eye in one of the War of Independence's naval battles; others claim it was a childhood accident. Still others say his wife gouged it for his infidelity—an unlikely blend of history and folklore.

Just below, I find an imposing front gate topped by an old turret with musket slits, guarding a vacant block enclosed by a high stone wall.

This is all that remains of Uncle Giorgios' house.

Donkeys clip-clop past, their wooden saddles as flat as boards—I guess because they *are* boards. No one could sit on them, surely, for more than 30 seconds.

Good for stacking goods, though. One even carries a double mattress—Hydra's version of 'free delivery'. Flowers aren't planted along these streets; the wind would tear them up in no time. But here and there, I spot a yellow freesia against a blue door, rambunctious red geraniums, chattering daisies.

Back at the port, I buy grass-fed steak grown on the Peloponnese from the local butcher, who does his best grumpy butcher impersonation.

John and I were proud of the pasture-fed beef we raised on our farm, so I'm curious to try the Greek version.

I also pick up some fresh vegetables from Pete.

As I walk home, I think about Ghikas.

What was his favourite meal. What were his passions? What motivated him? Who was this man, really? I wonder if he felt the same sense of purpose that John has always had. Did he see things in black and white, speaking out without hesitation? Or was he more thoughtful, weighing each decision carefully? He walked on these cobblestones; he lived, loved, and struggled here. Did he fight for his beliefs with quiet resolve, or was he bold and brash? Was he courageous?

Back at home, I find Skotádi waiting by my front door, once again insisting I'm the only human he has ever truly loved.

Today, he introduces me to one of his friends lounging on the ramparts—a striking pearl-grey beauty, a compact, furry bundle, her outline haloed in the dwindling sunlight. She squints at me with an almost aristocratic air as I snap her photo and attempt to strike up a conversation.

Clearly, she's seen it all, and her reaction is pure ennui.

As for the steak?

It's the toughest I've ever eaten.

I bet the butcher would perfect his grumpy impersonation if I told him that—but I won't.

At least Skotádi loves the leftovers.

The wind has dropped. I might look up some tips on writing historical fiction.

Or maybe I won't.

Hydra, with all its odd, endearing ways, is carving out a little space in my heart.

Méhri ávrio, filakária—until tomorrow, dear wandering buddies, it's *kalinίkta!*

6

HYDRAIKI AND KANTADA

The morning light streams into the apartment. I'm lucky I chose this side of the harbour, or it chose me.

Call it serious real estate karma.

The reason?

The sun doesn't warm my windows until 8 am, and the apartments on the other side of the port must wait until the afternoon—a disadvantage in winter, but surely a good reason to rent on that side in summer.

They say the sunsets are spectacular in summer, from any vantage point. There's even a restaurant here called Sunset—closed for the season, naturally. Nearby, Omilos sounds promising, but it's closed too.

Hydra is proud of its heroes from the War of Independence, so it's fitting that the bronze statue of the boy on the dolphin—the one from the 1957 Sophia Loren film—is almost hidden on the western bluff near the windmill, tucked quietly into the landscape. As if to say, 'Hollywood heroes are fun, but we have more impressive ones of our own'.

I salute these brave heroes, but right now my focus is firmly on my stomach. When a girl has to wait until 8am for sunrise, a little sustenance is essential to keep her strength up.

So I need to pop out for groceries, but there's a more pressing issue. The front door faces straight into the sea breeze, and the lock has been playing up. With Iliana in Athens and no Manjola to save me, if I were locked out, I'd be homeless on Hydra—a predicament I'd rather avoid. So it's off to the hardware shop for a tin of marine-grade lubricant spray.

I pass another grocery store with parsley on display. Gorgeous, freshly picked, effervescing bunches of deep green parsley! I almost check over my shoulder to make sure Pete isn't watching. So when I head to his shop for pepper and wine, I'm a bundle of nerves about the contraband in my hand. I rehearse my lines, "It wasn't anything you said, Pete, it was me." Or "The parsley made me do it."

Afterwards, I stop to watch the traffic in the harbour, imagining what Hydra must have been like in Ghikas' time—the naval powerhouse of the Mediterranean. But this dominance wasn't a gift from the gods. With Hydra's barren landscape, the islanders—originally Albanians fleeing Turkish oppression in the 1400-1500s—had to rely on the sea. So they became master shipbuilders by necessity. Every rocky cove became a shipyard, with each man learning the entire process of building a *hydraiki* from start to finish.

I used to think of Hydra as safe and impregnable, but after reading the story of Konstantine Sakellarios, my

Hydraiki and Kantada

perspective has shifted. Around the start of the 1800s, Barbary pirates from Algiers attacked Hydra—as sometimes happened—capturing Konstantine in the process. When he finally returned home—probably through his relatives paying ransom, but it took quite a while—he brought back the pirates' shipbuilding knowledge, turning lemons into lemonade!

His story makes me see Hydra differently. The islanders could never afford to relax their vigilance, and it explains why they stationed a lookout high above the town to warn of approaching threats. And with all those cannons still mounted around the harbour, it's clear that they weren't messing around—they were ready to defend their turf.

Piecing together Ghikas' story feels like building a ship—assembling something from scattered fragments and raw materials. I'm still approaching it as a task of recording my findings, jotting down notes, and gathering details. I find myself imagining his motives to fill in the gaps—not quite writing a book yet but trying to understand him better.

Back at the apartment, a few squirts on the lock, and *ópa*, problem solved—it clicks open and closed with satisfying precision. I can stop worrying about turning into the bag lady of Hydra. That's the thing about fixing a door—a few simple steps, and it's done. Is that what writing a book is like too? Keep going until you type '*the end*'?

I love history. I settle in at my desk and scroll through an online article about Hydra in the early 1800s—it was the Ottoman empire's spoiled child, governing itself but paying the price by being obliged to send its sons to serve in the Turkish navy, presumably to show them how it was *really* done.

It wasn't even part of what we think of as Greece today. Because Greece didn't exist until after the War of Independence. When Ghikas was in New South Wales.

The Greek War of Independence has become my bedtime reading. Primary sources—official records, first-hand accounts, letters—they're the best way to really connect with events. Thank goodness for The Grand Tour era, when the upper classes roamed Europe with a pen in one hand and a journal in the other. Now, thanks to Google Books, many of these travelogues are freely available.

Then there are the history books, piling up on my bedside table. They're subjective, secondary sources, but crucial to fleshing out the story. Over the last few months, they've arrived in such numbers that John and the mailman have bonded in a collaborative head-shaking routine.

I was trying to figure out how Ghikas fitted into all of this; where he belongs in the island's history.

With the fast internet connection urban living has brought, I've pieced together his story in brief. He was twenty-two when he arrived in Australia in 1829 as a convicted pirate, and he too became a land-holding grazier, the same as John and I.

But who was he before that? Here, on Hydra?

As I reflect, I become aware of the strains of bouzouki music drifting in the window—that unmistakable sound of Greece—carrying with it all the warmth and joy of a sunlit morning. The compelling, low, rolling waltz rhythm of guitar chords is overlaid by the high, bright, dancing notes of the bouzouki melody. One that makes you want to close your eyes, and sway from side to side, letting the rhythm wash over you.

Hydraiki and Kantada

I am lured to the window.

The sky is a blinding, brilliant blue. A line of fishing boats of all shapes and sizes is moored along the stone breakwater, blue and white Greek flags fluttering from their masts in the brisk breeze. The smooth water of the port laps against the hulls, each swell bouncing off as a ripple, almost in time with the music, ending as a gentle splash against the rocks. The only human movement comes from a man and his wife, working side by side, their conversation as fluid as the motion of their hands stringing yellow fishing nets out along the walkway. Overhead, seagulls wheel and cry, their calls intertwined with the bouzouki melody, while little *Sea Bird* darts in and out of the harbour, ferrying passengers along the coast. Everything is in perfect harmony.

I grab my iPhone, needing to capture this idyllic moment. I record a video—man, music, sea. I know I'll return to this thirty-second clip again and again—a memory of Hydra, a *kantada* (a Greek serenade sung in the streets) to carry with me wherever I go.

All the wrinkles have been ironed out of my soul.

I try to analyse the perfection of the scene I've just described. The architectural backdrop of whitewashed buildings helps—they cluster around the quay, anchored to the water's edge, while those perched on the hillsides blend seamlessly into the landscape as if they've grown from the mother rock itself. This harmony isn't accidental. It's been carefully preserved over centuries—Hydra's commitment to spartan simplicity is legislated. I read that a public building, funded by a benefactor early in the 20th century, was pulled down for being too ostentatious. On Hydra, even generosity must conform to severity.

Flashy is not a word they like here. Leave your bling at the door.

I push my sparkly shoes under the desk.

Excitement strikes late morning—my excitement, that is. A luxury yacht named *Glaros*, a behemoth compared to *Sea Bird*, is attempting to dock at the breakwater. The only berth left doesn't look nearly big enough for *Glaros*. A couple of old men (about my age! eek!) come to sit beneath my window to watch. One shakes his head and says something which I translate to mean, 'This will be a disaster."

His friend laughs, clearly enjoying the spectacle.

I hold my breath as the yacht inches backward, the gap narrowing dangerously. Finally, after several tense minutes, with frantic shouting from the dockhands who are running back and forth and gesticulating wildly on the breakwater, the *Glaros* squeaks in with inches to spare. My two men burst into applause, their laughter drifting upwards.

I google the *Glaros*—you can charter her for €85,000 a week. I can think of better things to do with my €85,000. If I ever find it.

When I need a break, and since there are no cream buns to be found here (another obsession!), I indulge in a waffle at Eileen's ice-cream shop on the corner near the Pirate Bar. Hot waffle + cold ice cream = utter bliss.

In the afternoon, I take a stroll to Kamini, a lovely kilometre along a stone-paved corso, with a steep drop at Avlaki to a stone diving platform at the water line below. The seat above is perfect for contemplating the meaning of life or admiring the view. *Sea Bird* makes a cameo appearance as usual—that little boat has a better social life than I do.

Hydraiki and Kantada

It's a glorious afternoon, warm enough to take off my jumper. This is winter on Hydra.

As I wander, I reflect on the creative minds—writers, artists, and musicians—who found inspiration here. Nikos Hadjikyriakos-Ghikas, an aristocratic painter influenced by Cubism and Surrealism, inherited his family's dilapidated 40-room mansion above Kamini. After renovations, he transformed it into a cultural hub for creatives worldwide, hosting luminaries like Henry Miller, Lawrence Durrell, Margot Fonteyn, Frederick Ashton, and Sidney and Cynthia Nolan. Miller described dining on the terrace as an experience "in drunken stupefaction," with guests leaving the table as full as "wine casks."

Sounds quite the party house!

Charmian Clift mentioned his home in *Peel Me a Lotus*. And Patrick Leigh Fermor said that without Hydra (and this house), his book, *Mani: Travels in the Southern Peloponnese* would never have been written. What a fine history of patronage of the arts!

I'm rather chuffed to think I might be treading, however humbly, in their footsteps. All I need now is an aristocrat to lend me a mansion for a year.

The (artist) Ghikas' mansion burned down in 1965, and it's said that he was so heartbroken he never returned. Now, it's a ruin. Another renowned Hydriot artist, Tetsis, whose work I greatly admire, lived in a far more modest house not far from the Ghikas mansion, and they were firm friends. His home, once his parents' residence and his grandparents' shop, is now a museum—though, of course, it's closed for the season.

Late in the afternoon as I'm strolling happily back to the

port, a woman wearing an apron pulls me up to ask if I know there's a festival tomorrow afternoon. She insists I must attend. How can I refuse? It's sure to be fun!

But the best news of the day? I finally spoke to Maria, the historian, on the phone. She's going to take us on a tour of Hydra on Wednesday. And wait for it—yes, she's a Voulgaris, and she believes she's related to Ghikas himself. The funny part is she can't wait to hear what her aunt has to say about Ghikas.

Aunt? Me? Fact really is stranger than fiction, isn't it?

Tomorrow and Monday are holidays, so I'll go back to the archives on Tuesday to see what Eleni has for me.

I've been writing for an hour straight tonight and absolutely loving it!

Méhri ávrio, until tomorrow, buddies.

7

APOKRIES SUNDAY

At dawn this morning, I forgot yet again about the pigeons next door. They use the terracotta roof as their personal penthouse, ignoring the fine wire fringing along the ledges as if it's decoration. I don't know who gets the bigger fright when I fling the windows open—me or the birds. With a great beating of wings, they rise into the air in a huff and fly off, leaving me standing there recovering from the shock. They don't come back until nightfall. I'm their daylight-saving monster.

I wish I could apologise.

Before lunch, I climb the eastern side of the harbour, up steep stone steps near the naval academy and explore the walkways up there, taking photos. Then I wind my way along the coastline a little way towards Mandraki. The gardens on Hydra have a wild charm, and the citrus crop is amazing. Pretty little flowers thrive in the cracks of the paving, adding bursts of colour to the grey stone. And oh, again, the water! The clarity of that enchanting blue looks too perfect to be real.

I pass a forbidding stone building perched solidly off the path on the cliff beside me—squat, with a flat concrete lid for a roof and no windows except for a small barred one set absurdly high. It has all the charm of a bomb shelter. I ask later—it's a slaughterhouse converted into a contemporary art exhibition space, run by the Deste Foundation, based in Athens. Only open of course in the summer months. Wish I could peek inside. There's something rather grotesque (and wonderfully appealing) about taking something macabre and repurposing it as an art gallery. A metaphor for modern art itself.

Back at the port, everywhere I turn, there are cats. Some wait for the fishing boats to be unloaded; others sleep where they please. A big ship is disgorging passengers for the carnival today—many pulling bags, making a long weekend by staying over for the public holiday tomorrow. One little girl is beyond thrilled to be riding a donkey.

Let me tell you about this afternoon. We are at the tail end of Apokries now—the Greek carnival season before Lent kicks in, with Easter to follow as the biggest religious festival of the year. But the carnival season has its roots in ancient pagan Greece, celebrating Dionysus, the god of wine, and the arrival of Spring. Although between you and me, I think Spring's still stuck somewhere out at sea.

It's a full-blown masquerade parade. Historically, it was the ultimate disguise party where you could lose your identity, toss out the rules of conduct, and swap genders in the blink of an eye—the one time of year you could be silly without being recognised. From what I saw, not much has changed. It's still a glorious excuse for adults to dress up and embrace their inner child—no judgment allowed.

The festivities kick off at 2:30pm at Votsis Square. When I arrive, the band is already playing, and people are milling about in flamboyant costumes, exclaiming over each other's outrageous outfits.

The procession is a hilarious mock wedding party, and the children are decked out as their favourite cartoon characters, while the adults embrace their inner pirates, packs of cards, and sponge divers. The lead is a donkey, hilariously outfitted with speakers, making it the most rustic mobile sound system I've ever seen. Following behind is the spirit of the festival, a colourful character who sets the tone for the rest of the parade. Next comes the bride and groom—though I must say, I've never seen a bride quite like this one. Picture an aging man in a wedding dress, with chest hair sprouting from a plunging neckline, and you get the idea. The bridesmaids, played by children and hilariously pretend-pregnant teenagers, hold the bride's train, adding to the carnival atmosphere.

The guest list is just as eclectic—an artist, a scullery maid, and a bunny, all mingling with more packs of cards and even a few pirates. One particularly sweet child, eager for a photo, nods vigorously when I ask for permission from her mother, while a dog up on a balcony desperately tries to join the fun, tail wagging furiously.

Among the other participants, two Mexicans, complete with sombreros, add a splash of international flavour; a man-sized cigarette is talking on his mobile phone. And then there's the group of pirates, with a grandpa who looks like he's been sailing the seven seas for centuries.

The parade also features a wizard who gives a cheerful thumbs up, Princess Blue, and even Mimi from the shop across the harbour, all dressed to the nines. One standout is a genuine sponge diver's suit from the 20th century, reminiscent of Sophia Loren in "Boy on a Dolphin."

It's a riot of pure fun. As the parade winds through the cobbled streets, I find myself swept up in the all-in enthusiasm for Apokries. The locals' laughter and the children's delighted shrieks make me feel, if only for a moment, like a Hydriot.

But practicality wins out. I don't follow the whole route of the procession, as they march around the back of town, along the hills to Kamini, with stops here and there, and then back along the coast, ending a couple of hours later back at the harbour with a live band, where the wedding ceremony begins. I enjoy their return to the port from my bedroom window, the 1958 song "Tequila" blaring out, and laughter drifting on the evening breeze. Even Long John Silver and his moll are making an appearance, adding to the delightful chaos.

Watching the passing parade, I think about Klein's musings on the importance of play, especially as we get older. He believes that play isn't only for children but is a way for us to stay young at heart. Here, looking at grown men dressed as brides and children as pirates, I can see that this community hasn't forgotten how to play. We should all learn how to embrace silliness again, to let go of our usual roles and enjoy ourselves without overthinking. Throw away the expectations we often lay on ourselves?

I wander down to the quay to watch the dancing, content in my role as a spectator. The circle of dancers swells, contracts, and spins, skirts swishing in a blur of colour. The energy pulses through the crowd. I begin to record it on video with my phone, the music loud in the air.

As I swing the phone around to capture the enthusiasm of the spectators, a woman on a bench catches my attention. Her eyes are locked on the dancers with an intensity that's hard to miss. At first, she claps and watches, leaning into the rhythm, but then something shifts. Suddenly, she's on her feet, undoing the belt and buttons of her coat and hurling it at her seat with urgency. She dance-steps into the circle, to be instantly absorbed by the other dancers.

It's a moment of pure spontaneity and joy—one I want to hold onto forever. A part of me longs to jump in, to be swept up in the music and laughter. There was a time when I would have joined without hesitation, but now, I find a different kind of joy in simply watching from the sidelines. It's not just about being content with observation; I'm as connected to the energy of the moment as if I were in the thick of it. I don't need to keep up with the pace or worry about disrupting the dance. I'm at peace with where I am, and I think Klein would approve.

Is this what being a writer means? Finding fulfilment not in the spotlight but in the quiet act of observation, of capturing the stories that others live?

When I leave around five, the music is still picking up pace, and even now, I can hear the happy tunes through my open window—a reminder that life's dance continues, whether I'm in the circle or not.

Tomorrow is Clean Monday or *Katheri Deftera*. I thought it must be a rubbish collecting day like our Clean Up Australia Day. But no, it's a public holiday—when souls are cleaned and purified after Apokries, ready for the Lenten fast. People fly homemade kites down the coast at Vlychos Beach. I'll take a sea taxi!

Apokries means goodbye meat, the same as carnival: 'carne' = meat, 'vale' = goodbye. But fish and shellfish are allowed—tomorrow the restaurants will serve seafood. A good excuse to eat out, as if I need one. I think of our son, who's a fantastic cook—his favourite dish is a Thai-flavoured chilli crab, and I love the way he puts the bold, fragrant spices together.

Maria texts to say she is going to meet me under the clock tower at 11am on Tuesday.

I've enjoyed writing about Apokries for you tonight.

Aftó ítan gia símera, fíli. That's it for today, buddies.

8

THE OLIVE TREE AND THE WHITE CAT

Today is a brisk 4°—9°C, which might sound chilly, but with barely a whisper of wind, it's surprisingly mild. I was busy writing last night and forgot to eat, so at 2am I cooked a plate of steamed vegetables and slathered them with butter. Of course, after that, I didn't want breakfast.

Did I say I forgot to eat? Funny, that hasn't happened in a long while.

I head up to Kiafa, the oldest part of Hydra, aptly named "top" for its high vantage point above a small cliff. The early Albanian settlers built their stone houses up here and connected them with arched stone bridges and covered passageways, perfect for defence against attack. By the late 1600s, Kiafa was a tightly packed cluster of homes with narrow windows for musket fire and flat roofs that doubled as battlements.

I almost hear the shouted warnings about approaching pirates, men loading muskets to defend their homes, mothers calling their children inside, and the slam of bolts on these old doors.

On the high terraces, I stumble upon a truly venerable olive tree. Its thick, gnarled trunk is twisted and contorted, with deep cracks and crevices, evidence of its age and endurance. The branches, trimmed hard over the years, sprout in frantic bunches from the top, thin and springy, stretching skyward in a bid for survival. This isn't just a tree; it's a living symbol of Hydra itself—stubborn, resilient, and shaped by the passage of time. I wonder if it has been here since Ghikas' day.

The squashed black fruits I've noticed on the stone stairs of the town suddenly make sense—they're olives, casualties of backyard trees. Prickly pears thrive, and the fruit is nearly ripe. Tall trees are scarce, with only a few straggly pines finding purchase in the rocky soil.

The steep streets leading down to the sea can turn into lethal torrents during heavy rains, which required the Hydriots to build their walkways high along the sides of the ravines. Their house walls are thicker at the base to resist erosion, and entrances face away from the water flow. Practical people.

The whitewashed houses now range from large, smart, refurbished villas with glossy enamel doors in bright colours (although some colours are forbidden) and smart new hardware, to houses with peeling paint and rotting wood, and even ruins. It's the consistency in architectural style that gives the entire town such perfect harmony. There's a church at nearly every turn, most boarded up. Among them is Saint Constantine's—remember, I promised to find it? It's located on the very plot of land where his family originally lived.

The Olive Tree and the White Cat

His is a sad story.

Born on Hydra in 1770, when the island was under Ottoman rule, Constantine grew up in a strict Orthodox Christian home, up here on Kiafa. Ignoring his mother's warnings, he left for Rhodes at 18 to work for the Turkish governor. After a wild night of drinking there, he ended up converting to Islam and was circumcised—whether tricked or simply too drunk to protest, no one knows. Consequently, he was shunned by his Christian friends and when he returned to Hydra, his mother disowned him. Eventually, he made his way back to Rhodes to renounce his conversion. The Turks tortured and hanged him in 1800, when he was 30 years old.

Such commitment to one's beliefs. Such cruel times.

The ornate clock tower or *kambanarió* next to Saint Constantine's church shrieks against Hydra's otherwise severe architecture, yet it matches the other bell towers in town. I wonder if they were built by travelling craftsmen—Venetian? Genoese?—who knew only one design. Cheaper by the dozen?

Because the door is locked, I press my phone flat against the window—my 21st-century keyhole into the past. I think the fresco tableau of iconography on the walls tells the story of his martyrdom.

I sense someone watching me—you know that uncanny feeling, a prickling at the back of your neck, when you know someone's watching. Isn't it strange how you can sense it, even in a crowd? The hairs stand up, and suddenly you're hyper-aware, scanning the scene for that unseen spectator. Unsettling, isn't it?

I turn. Behind me, on a high rock wall above me,

eyeballing me, is an inscrutable white cat. He's staring at me in the same way I've observed the Hydriots watch tourists and strangers—not with hostility, but with a mix of curiosity and quiet reserve. They are cautious with outsiders, like this cat. I've been blown away by their warmth, but it's a gentle reminder that, as a visitor, I am always under a watchful eye evaluating if I truly understand and respect the island's unique spirit and history.

Hunger drives me back down to the harbour, where, at the end of the 1700s, wealthy shipowners started building their massive, fortified mansions up the steep, rocky hills— no pile drivers or cranes in those days. These shipowners weren't just captains of the sea, but engineers and master builders too. Or, more likely, they knew exactly who to hire.

Houses now stretch from Kiafa down to the harbour and are crammed into every space between.

I climb the wooden stairs again to Psarapoula. Ilias is out on the balcony. He smiles with warmth in his eyes.

"Are you open, Ilia?"

Did you know that when you address a Greek directly, that you drop the 's' on their name? So Ilias becomes Ilia. Andonis becomes Andoni. Ghikas becomes Ghika.

He laughs. "Not yet. It's only 11:30."

I laugh too and descend the stairs—I am clearly *not* running on Hydra time. Halfway down, I run into Eileen coming out of her side door—her apartment is above her ice-cream shop. "They're not open," I say pointing up at Psarapoula. "But my stomach says it's lunchtime!"

"Come with me," she says. "You need a snack to keep you going. I'll give you a piece of cake. My sister made it." Cake perfection! She refuses when I try to pay.

The Olive Tree and the White Cat

On my way past Spiros' jewellery store, he comes out to ask what I am doing. "Going home till lunchtime," I say.

"You know you eat seafood today, for Clean Monday, don't you?' he asks. "You should go to Kontilenia at Kamini. It's a tavern specialising in fish, owned by my friend Dimitris. It's a wonderful tavern. It's perfect! You must go there! Tell him Spiros sent you."

I recognise the name—it's Klein's favourite restaurant, where he sat observing the old men at Kamini. And he loves Dimitris. How can I resist—the weather is less than ideal for kite-flying at Vlychos. I write for an hour, then I enjoy the brisk kilometre walk along the coast, looking forward to lunch. I round a corner and spread out below me is a view of a little marina; beside me, the outdoor terrace of the taverna. There are few patrons yet—I'm still too early?

I introduce myself to Dimitris. Then I say, "May I see the menu please?"

Underwhelmed by my request, and by my attendance, he points at the display cabinet. "That's the menu. You choose." He's had a big festival too. Or there's never been a menu.

The fish with tomato and capers looks perfect for Clean Monday. And it comes with chips! The wine is decanted into an anodised cup from the restaurant's barrel for me to pour into my wine glass. It's surprisingly good. I choose a seat on the edge of the terrace to watch the water taxis whizzing in and out, and the few men tinkering with their boats.

The acid of the capers perfectly balances the oil of the fish. Plus, a little Greek side salad of tomato, green capsicum, onion, bitter olives, cucumber, and the most delicious, herbed feta on top. As I eat, the cold begins to seep into my bones.

The website said Dimitris will phone a taxi for you. So when I've finished, I ask if he will ring *Sea Bird*, please. *Sea Bird* doesn't answer his phone—he's taking a well-deserved rest too, I guess. Then Dimitris notices a water taxi at the small dock in front of the peeling two-storey ochre and oxblood coloured building, about to back out. He gives a huge wolf whistle right in my ear, and I scoot down the stone steps, across the sandy beach, and up onto the dock. Rain is starting to fall. The trip home takes less than five minutes.

Hydra is deserted again. Everyone has gone back to the mainland, and the drizzle is falling. On the walk home from the taxi rank, I see Sassa, who says she has a headache from last night but what fun it was. Eileen waves from inside her shop, and then I pop in to see Vaso, who says she's going to Tsarapoula for dinner with a friend.

My little apartment welcomes me back like an old friend who always knows what to say. It's nice to be sitting at the computer typing, listening to the soft patter of drizzle against the window, feeling no need for dinner. Hydra feels different today—quiet, almost introspective, compared to the lively buzz of the past few days. The stillness wraps around me like a well-worn sweater on a chilly day—as if the island itself is pausing to gather its thoughts.

Clean Monday is a time for cleansing souls and giving up meat for Lent. The island is gathering itself, not only for Easter but for the inevitable summer tourist rush. There's a rhythm to this preparation—like the olives on the stairs, it's about sweeping up what's fallen—gathering what's been scattered or lost in day-to-day life. And somehow, without even thinking about it, I'm pausing too, taking stock of what I've come here to do. What am I giving up? My doubts, my uncertainty. Gathering creativity in a moment of stillness, allowing my thoughts to settle before the next burst of writing inspiration.

But I realise there's a fine line between floating in a sea of calm preparing to act—and drifting aimlessly. Maybe this is what Klein was getting at—finding fulfilment not in reaching the end, but in staying focussed on the process, yet still moving forward, even at a snail's pace. Then it's not work, but a joy.

I'll leave you with the words of the Greek writer Odysseus Elytis, who won the Nobel Prize for Literature in 1979:

"If you deconstruct Greece, you will, in the end, see an olive tree, a grapevine, and a boat."

I haven't seen any grapevines yet—plenty of the other two, though. But now I am playing with his sentence. Something like:

"Greece is built on three pillars: the resilience of the olive tree, the fecundity of the grapevine, and the bounty of the sea."

No. Not that.

Even more simple: "To understand Greece, one must taste its olives, drink its wine, and sail its seas."

No, no. I prefer his version. That's why he's a Nobel Prize winner.

Anyway, that's enough writerly activity for now.

Until tomorrow, buddies, *sas periméno*. I wait you.

9

FOR THE LOVE OF WRITING

Each night, I close the heavy wooden shutters to keep in the warmth. Each morning, when I open them, I never know what weather will be. Today, cold grey fog glowers from the tops of the mountains behind the town, draining all colour from the landscape. Showers scud across the port. A few people chat in small huddles under awnings or hug the sides of the buildings. I'm glad to be inside.

The flags on the boats stretch out in the wind. Most fly the Greek flag in blue and white, and some also fly the flag of Hydra. Introduced around the time of the revolution, it's full of symbolism of the struggle for independence of the Hydriots against the Ottoman Turks. A large cross in the middle represents Orthodox Christianity, the pole pushed into the crescent of Islam below. Political alliances in those days, indeed even today, often fell along religious lines, but at its core, the War of Independence was about reclaiming freedom from an oppressive power. That's the background to

Hydra's, and perhaps Ghikas' story—the human desire for freedom, with religion as the backdrop.

The inscription on the crescent is the battle cry of Spartan mothers who said to their sons, "Come back from battle *with* your shield, or come back *on* it." In other words, come back triumphant or don't come back.

Some male historian made that up.

But I want to channel that same stubborn Hydriot defiance, that refusal to yield, into researching Ghikas' story.

It's time for us to go out to the archives again—and I really love this chill in the air once I'm rugged up. Let's hope we see Mrs. Adamopoulou, the boss, to discuss what might still be in the archives that didn't turn up the other day and ask where we might look next. And Eleni might have the information about the Herakles. Or she might have found the book.

"May I make an appointment?" I ask.

"Perhaps she'll be in after 1pm," Stam says. "Come then."

I go upstairs to give Eleni two names she requested the other day. She happily searches again, finds more inconclusive information.

I have an appointment with Maria, my husband's cousin, the historian, at 11am. "May I come back this afternoon?" I ask Eleni, hopeful she might find the Papamanolis book.

"I won't be here. Tomorrow morning will be better," she says.

"Right," I say.

I am waiting at the clock tower at 11am, when my phone rings. It's Maria. "I'm coming, I'm coming!"

I realise I left my portable power bank back at the archives. I need to recharge it.

As Maria walks towards me, I am struck by her beauty—long raven hair, beautiful dark eyes, fair skin, a dazzling smile. She kisses me on both cheeks.

"It's good to meet you!" we both say at the same time.

"You are family!" she says.

Maria inherited her father's deep love of history. After studying in Athens for six years, she returned to Hydra as a teacher, historian and now guide, to live where her heart is. But she may return to Athens to do another degree. She has a brother and a sister, but she lives alone—she doesn't mention a boyfriend.

We go to her cousin's restaurant and coffee shop, Sinialo, for a coffee. I am welcomed and exclaimed over, with two more cousins hugging me as well. They don't distinguish between real rellies and in-laws like me.

Maria and I don't draw breath. She is excited at my research, my book, and almost claps her hands in delight at the places it is taking me. I'm living her dream. I'm living my own!

She is researching the mansions of Hydra, which will take her until May. She tells me how generous the island's powerful families have been. The Tsamados family donated their mansion to house the Maritime Academy; the Athens School of Fine Arts has a branch in the Tombazi mansion, and the Kountouriotis family gifted their mansion to the Historic-Ethnologic Institute of Greece, and it opens as a branch of the National Museum of History. In the summer Maria will have time, she thinks, to research my subject, both here and in Athens, where she is sure she will find information. "I will send it to you, translated," she says. "It will be wonderful for my research, too. Perhaps I will write a history book, while you write your novel." A collaboration!

Her passion for history reminds me of Klein's idea that it's beneficial to surround yourself with wise people with good stories.

Her enthusiasm is infectious, and for the first time, I am more than a curious traveller—I'm a writer with a real project. This is no longer a personal quest; it's turning into something bigger, something shared. I must get this story right.

While we have a photo call on the footpath—Maria, her cousins and me—a vehicular ferry usually moored at the dock is being unloaded of its cargo of donkeys, who march off with all the nonchalance of seasoned travellers. I suppose they're all related to each other as well!

I arrange to meet Maria tomorrow at 11am for our tour, and we'll have a meal together before I leave the island.

When she leaves, it's time for lunch at Piato. Customers use restaurant pens to design their plates, which are then displayed—today, there are many more plates than customers. I suppose during 'the season', the place is so busy you'd have trouble being served.

Yia-yia Katerina says, "I've made some octopus pasta. Would you like some?"

"What about dolmades?" I ask. "Eileen says you make wonderful dolmades!"

Katerina laughs. "Yes, Eileen likes them very much!"

So do I.

I've always been hesitant to try Greek dolmades again—thanks to a sad, grey, bottled version I once had at home, which I thought had put me off them for life. But these? These are a revelation—light, stuffed with perfectly seasoned mince, and bathed in a rich, lemony sauce. I give my belly a pat.

I go back to the Archives at about 2pm as Stam suggested —but Mrs Adamopoulou is not there. Neither is Stam. The woman behind the desk wishes I weren't either.

"Perhaps tomorrow morning," she says in a monotone, rolling the 'r' in "tomorrrrrrrow" and drawing out the "mawwwwwwning".

The "mawwwwwning" slides off the desk and rolls underneath it somewhere.

"What time?" I ask, with a polite smile. "May I make an appointment?"

She shrugs and turns down her mouth. I feel a flicker of irritation. But maybe I should slow down. Or pretend to.

I try again. "When shall I come to see her?"

Another shrug. "We open at 10."

I wonder if Mrs Adamopoulou knows how elusive she is. Or is this woman trying to be difficult?

"I'm awfully sorry, but I left my power bank up in the archives this morning," I say, hoping to strike a more conciliatory tone.

She sighs, a clear sign of exasperation. I can almost hear her thinking "Oh, for god's sake. They're CLOSED." But she doesn't voice it.

I give her my best pleading look. "I'm sorry, I need to recharge it before tomorrow."

Her eyes roll backwards. She grabs some keys—probably planning to lock me in a cupboard—and starts up the stairs, muttering. I traipse along before she changes her mind.

When she unlocks the door, there it is, to my immense relief, right where I left it.

'Thank you, thank you,' I gush, overdoing it a bit.

As I walk out the door, I start to wonder—maybe I'm a bit too intense. Or maybe she's allergic to people.

I go looking for that shop, Spoiled, and find it. Closed—for the season, or for lunch? I'll find out tomorrow. An Oscar Wilde quote on the front door explains the name: "All charming people, I fancy, are spoiled. It is the secret of their attraction."

Well, if Wilde is right, judging from what happened at the archives, I've got a lot of work to do on myself. A slab of almond crunch should do the trick.

Later, I look up the quote and find it's from *The Portrait of Mr. W. H...*

I stumble upon another gem from the same work: "It is always a silly thing to give advice, but to give good advice is absolutely fatal." What a comic genius.

The tourist shops are full of *mati* (*matiasma* or the evil eye) jewellery and curios—the older generation still believe in it, but for the rest, it's more about decoration and tradition—bunches of garlic dangle over entrance doors.

It's been a great day, hasn't it? Maria is such a treasure—not just because of her charm, warmth, and generosity, which make her a wonderful relative to discover—she's a fantastic ambassador for the island.

Speaking of finds, I haven't mentioned the flurry of emails back and forth from the Englishman on the plane. For a ship's captain, he makes a fine historical researcher! Am I not blessed?

I was about to say, "I wait you." I've said it before, and

you probably thought it was a typo. But there's actually a story behind it—let me explain.

Back in Istanbul in 2015, I asked a towering young man taking tickets for the double-decker tourist bus when the next one would leave. We wanted to grab lunch but didn't want to miss the departure. His navy T-shirt revealed one heavily tattooed arm—something I find intimidating—yet he had the poise of a modern-day Janissary, one of those elite Ottoman warriors chosen for their courage and splendid physique from all the regions of the empire. His deep brown eyes were warm, and with a magnetic smile that flashed strong, uneven white teeth, he said in a rich accent, "Pleez. Go. Buy your lunch."

Perhaps I hesitated, because then he *really* looked into my eyes, as if no one else in the world existed. "Don't worry. Go. I wait you."

He smiled again.

Extraordinary.

How could I ever forget that?

I've thought about that moment many times since and wonder why I remember it so clearly. Maybe because it was a moment of absolute trust between strangers—he trusted I'd hurry back, and I trusted he'd hold the bus. Amazing how trust can be built in a second.

And isn't it strange how, out of all the millions of minutes in a lifetime, only a few are branded indelibly into our minds? Some go unnoticed only to surface later, triggered by a smell, a song, or some random remark—as if someone hit play on a reel we didn't know we were carrying. Some are warm and fuzzy—I suddenly picture the early morning my husband serenaded me in bed with 'Lazy Bones,' spectacularly out of tune—no wonder the choir master banned him. Or our two children on school holidays, playing on blow-up li-lows in the creek below the house, shrieking and laughing as they push each other off. Both my chicks safe and sound.

Others are weird random flashes that make no sense.

And then there are the ones we'd pay to forget—the 'please delete' moments. I'm sure you have yours. I do too.

Here on Hydra, I feel I'm in the middle of one of those rare precious times. Knowing that writing is waiting for me at the end of each day feels like a delicious indulgence. Shaping thoughts into sentences and sentences into paragraphs has become the heartbeat of my days.

It's another way of holding on to a moment.

I'm also really looking forward to our tour tomorrow.

Méchri tóte, fíli, sas periméno. Until then, buddies, I wait you.

10

IT'S ALL AMYGDALOTA TO ME

Thankfully, the weather is holding this morning for our visit to the archives and our tour with Maria. I want to be there on the dot of ten to see Mrs Adamopoulou, before she becomes busy.

On my way, I pass Eileen's shop, where two men are shifting the tables. Striding, pointing, measuring, indicating, disagreeing.

"We have this event every year," she says, laughing, "and every year there's a fight about how to arrange the tables." She stands with her arms crossed, looking on as if this is her favourite sitcom. She's letting the day roll out at its own pace. Just watching. There's no rush.

Along the dock, the usual lineup of cats has gathered to watch the fishing boats unloading, a picture of patience, waiting for their morning tea. No rush there either.

At 10am I enter the door of the archives, slightly more cautious.

'Yassas Stam,' I say, thinking myself very Greek.

"Yassas.' He smiles back with his usual cheerfulness.

Before I can ask, he jumps in. "I'm sorry about yesterday. Mrs Adamopoulou had to go to Athens. She's not back yet. Tomorrow. Maybe." He shrugs in a way that says, "This is Hellas. What can you do?"

The thought flits across my mind that they don't want me to speak with Mrs. Adamopoulou—or I've been blacklisted. I dismiss both as ridiculous.

"Is Eleni in yet please, Stam?" I ask. 'She told me to come back this morning.'

"No, not yet, but she should only be a few minutes. We'll turn on the lights for you."

"Thank you Stam. I'll wander a little while I wait."

As I turn to climb the stairs, my friend from yesterday comes out of an office with a warm smile to show Stam she has known me and liked me forever. I give her a warm smile back. She was busy yesterday. Maybe she was saying, "Slow down, stranger. We don't rush here."

Stam introduces her before she goes into the control room to turn on the lights. She's another Eleni.

Upstairs, I look at the large-scale model ships suspended from the ceiling. The details are perfect, and I wonder how many thousands of hours it took to make them. And how much glue.

A photo of one would be handy when I'm writing the book. No one is watching. The temptation to take a forbidden photo is strong. I know I shouldn't, but I'm about to raise my iPhone. The Greek chorus, ever-present in the back of my mind, whispers softly: 'Foolish mortal, why do you always test the gods? Why break the rules and then wonder why you are punished?"

Almost immediately I hear the door to the archives being unlocked. Saved from my sin. I turn and follow the sound.

Eleni comes around the corner, smiling. 'Good morning, Shelley,' she says. "It's nice to see you today."

"It's nice to see you too, Eleni," I say, relieved.

Yesterday, I suggested to her that perhaps Ghikas had named some of his children after his mother or father and perhaps we can trace him that way. I've brought back the names. Eleni checks the catalogue and opens book after book.

While she is looking, I ask if I may look on the bookshelves. "Perhaps a picture book?" I say, feeling silly. Who asks for picture books in a historical archive?

Eleni goes straight to a shelf and pulls out a book for me. "This one has pictures!"

She goes back to work. It's a modern publication about the heroes of the War of Independence with glossy photos of old paintings. I ask if I may take photos.

"No," she says, smiling, raising her index finger to her lips.

She keeps searching until nearly eleven.

"No," she says, "don't go. Maria will wait. Let me print this for you.'

She has found information about a ship called the Herakles! She knows who owned it—Anagnostis Papamanolis and Dimitris Georgiou Voulgaris—a future prime minister of Greece and probably Ghikas' first cousin—so a connection. The captain was Lazaros Papamanolis—related to the man who wrote the book? It was 31 piches long—Eleni thinks that could be a cubit, which is .75 metre or about 30 inches long—so about 23 metres. The page also has columns for wages paid, costs of repairs, and even cannons fitted (2).

Eleni kindly makes me a photocopy of these findings. This Herakles seems a bit too big for a crew of only nine, but it's hard to ignore the name Papamanolis appearing again. It's not impossible, but... I feel a sneaking excitement.

I text Maria to say I'll be a couple of minutes late, as I would if I were at home. But then I realise Maria won't even be thinking about where I am. On island time, a few minutes doesn't matter. Everyone knows you'll show up eventually.

Eleni hands me a sheet of paper with a translation of Ghikas' story. The narrative is the same as mine, but interestingly, a couple of details are slightly different. More for me to cross-check. I thank Eleni and hug her. She really is a darling.

But we're only scratching the surface. I'm still not sure if THE Nicholaos was Ghikas' father. If we could only find a copy of the Papamanolis book, a translation might tell me. But I'm not leaving Hydra empty-handed—I know much more than I did before I left home. The whole search process is addictive and thrilling.

Like Cinderella, I bolt down the stairs as the clock strikes the hour. Thankfully, my shoes stay on. As I run out of the archives, I see the tiny figure of Maria under the clock tower. She returns my wave.

We walk together out along the small stone apron, boats moored on either side. She gestures for me to sit on a bench while she remains standing. Initially nervous, she soon slips into a fascinating and well-rehearsed talk. I'm as captivated by her elegant delivery as by the history she's sharing.

She starts with the Albanian settlers who first made their

home on this barren, rocky island, then moves on to the Venetians, followed by the Ottoman Turks. Hydra's fortunes rose in the early 1800s, as the islanders became wealthy through shipping and trade, playing a pivotal role in the War of Independence. She points to the grand mansions built during that time and then gestures toward a large, empty block, enclosed by stone walls, where the Voulgaris mansion once stood—the entry turret I saw the other day. It was pulled down in the early 20th century. I know the family had given it to the island, and that it was Ottoman in style, and I can't help but wonder if that had something to do with its destruction.

Was it political? After the War of Independence, perhaps anything that looked Ottoman reminded the Hydriots of a time when they weren't in control of their own destiny. And with tensions still high between Greece and Turkey during World War I and the subsequent Balkan Wars, maybe an Ottoman-style mansion felt like a symbol of the past they were trying to leave behind. By the 1920s, when Greece was pushing into former Ottoman lands, perhaps anything linked to Turkish influence was considered an unwelcome relic—better off demolished.

Or maybe it was more practical—maybe it was falling apart. Too much rot, too many cracks. But then, why is the block still vacant? Why didn't they sell it? It seems odd for such prime land to remain untouched for such a long time.

I decide not to ask. Some things are better left unsaid. I'm turning Hydriot.

We visit the cathedral—the Church of the Assumption of the Virgin Mary—the one under the clock tower that I visited the other day on George's recommendation. Despite its size it's jam-packed with treasures. I'm always fascinated by the different ways the Virgin Mary is portrayed. Each icon of her has its own unique expression—sometimes she appears serene, other times sorrowful, and occasionally, and my favourites, joyful.

Maria says Napoleon gave the silver chandelier to Hydra for services in running the British blockade during the Napoleonic Wars. Others say the Hydriots stole it. -:)

The original church was destroyed by an earthquake in the eighteenth century, and it was rebuilt by Venetian artisans.

"Do you still have earthquakes?" I ask.

"No."

She will not allow it. What a relief.

I still haven't found out the significance of the two-headed eagle. I keep forgetting to ask—there was a two-headed-eagle cushion in the church as well as the marble plaque outside.

The entire background to the altar is made of carved marble. Did I tell you that the monks' cells of the cloisters at one stage became the island's prison? The compound was the town's meeting place during the War of Independence, and now it's the island's administration centre. The church has always been the centre of the town in more ways than one.

We walk around to the other side of the harbour and Maria describes how the Hydriots gave their all to the war effort, expecting to be rewarded with political appointments at independence. How it didn't happen, and how the admiral of their navy, their beloved Admiral Miaoulis again, in 1831, seized and ordered the destruction of the three main warships of the Greek fleet—Hellas, Hydra, and Spetsai—and they were burned to the waterline—preventing them from falling into the hands of the faction loyal to Governor Kapodistrias, who intended to sell them to the Russians to consolidate his finances and weaken the navy. What a story is that!

I said I'd tell you the one I like best about Admiral Miaoulis. It goes like this: During the English blockade of Europe to starve Napoleon out, Admiral Nelson captured Miaoulis' ship and took him captive. Nelson asked the Greek captain, "What would you do if you were in my position?"

Without missing a beat, Miaoulis boldly replied, "I would hang you."

Impressed by Miaoulis' courage and honesty, Nelson let him go.

As Maria talks about Hydra's fight against the Ottomans, I admire these islanders. They knew their enemy and stood their ground, no matter the odds.

Writers face an enemy too—the blank page, the critic, the doubt. Here I am, captivated by Ghikas' story but waffling over whether I have the right to tell it.

The sweetest revenge for Hydra though, was that five prime ministers after the war ended were Hydriots. One of them was Maria's great-great-great-grandfather Dimitris, a cousin of our hero. Part-owner of the Herakles Eleni found the other day.

"See his big nose?" Maria says, when she shows me his bas-relief face on the memorial to the five. "Like my father.'

When she was a little girl, if she spoke back to her father, he'd twirl his big moustache with his fingers, and say, pretending to be stern, "Do not speak back to me, young lady. I am the great-great grandson of a prime minister."

We pass the naval academy—I think of Panagiotis—training sea captains since 1749. A plaque on the wall says that a sea captain must be brave and virtuous.

"My sister is a sea captain," says Maria proudly. "And her husband."

They live on another island. And her brother is a trained sommelier at a resort along the coast.

I think of John at home on his surfboard.

We come to a plaque for a man called Nikolaos Giorgios Kolmaniatis.

"Oh, this is a great story," says Maria.

Nikolaos was a Hydriot ship's captain conscripted into the Turkish navy in the early 1800s. While he was away, he heard his wife was dallying with another man. He sailed home and shot the man dead and was sentenced to death himself for the murder. He made a run for it on a family ship, ending up in Argentina where he became a rear-admiral and a hero of the Argentinian war of independence against Spain. Evita Péron sent this plaque to Hydra in recognition of his place in Argentinian history.

"My boyfriend was a sea captain too, but I'm still alive."

She has a delightful laugh.

"Do you have a boyfriend now?" I ask.

"No, I'm free."

At the end of the tour, Maria gives me a pretty box containing *amygdalota* from her aunt's bakery. I'll take it home to try later because I tried *amygdolata* the other day and it was bland and tasteless. I don't want to have to be insincere if I try it now.

Maria's family home, her father's villa, is at Kamini. I ask her about the price of houses here.

"Out of reach," she says, "The most expensive real estate in Greece."

"How much would a wreck of a house be?"

"Millions," she says, "or billions!"

I show her a photo of a dog with his paws over the parapet wall of a house near the start of the festival—he's dying to join in.

"That's my apartment!" says Maria delightedly. "And that's my dog!"

I smile and shake my head at yet another coincidence.

On the way home, I take a photo that seems to capture the essence of Hydra, a study in pale blue: a small, pale blue fishing boat trailing a wake across a matching sea, set against the soft blue of the mainland and a pale blue sky filled with fluffy white clouds.

As I write this afternoon, recalling what we've uncovered in the archives and what Maria has told me, the rain comes down properly, with the occasional clap of thunder—not a wild tropical storm like I'm used to at home, but Hydra's gentler version of it. Now and then, the sun peeks through, to show there's no malice, before the next shower arrives. Eventually, it clears up, leaving bigger fluffier clouds in a bright blue sky.

I go for a walk to see if Spoiled is open. It's not. I buy supplies at Pete's.

My watch tells me I can complete my step target for today if I take a 15-minute walk. It's such a smart alec, that watch.

It's almost sunset and I walk around the headland. The

closed cafés with their stacks of chairs make nice abstract photos. There isn't a sunset tonight but the silver scene in the fading light is breathtaking. In the distance, I see Dokos, the island where the Hydriots quarried their stone. The little closer island looks as if it has a white tent on it, but I've heard it's a church, popular for weddings.

As I walk up the stairs to my front door, my watch congratulates me.

At my desk again, as I write, I'm no longer a tourist photographer with a notebook—I'm writing with a purpose. I'm learning to trust my voice, to let go of perfection, and find beauty in the rough edges of my prose. I'm enjoying writing down my reflections.

Klein would say that reflection is a powerful tool for understanding our past decisions and finding peace with them, I think. I see now that John spotted my new obsession before I did, which was why he gave me the plane ticket. How generous—and clever—of him to make my choice simple. His mother used to say, "Tether the dragon with a silken thread," meaning she thought John needed gentle handling. I took her advice. And John has turned her wisdom on me. His quiet encouragement has always been my anchor. In a world where dreams sometimes seem impossible, he has never once asked me to give mine up. Instead, he gives me the freedom to run after them, knowing that in allowing me to fly, he keeps me close.

And his loyalty is as strong as his will.

But he and I have always had a battle of wills, a constant juggle for dominance—with either one of us giving way now and then—but mostly me, for the sake of peace. Was that how Ghikas and Mary were? I haven't told you about her yet

—Ghikas' wife. She arrived in New South Wales as a 15 or 16-year-old orphan girl from Ireland, a free settler on an English government-funded ship meant to supply domestic servants—and, let's face it, wives—to the colony. Imagine crossing the world at such a young age. Things must have been desperate in Cork, or maybe an adventurous streak drove her.

I wonder how they met. Was it an instant attraction, or a marriage of convenience? Did she and Ghikas clash in the same way John and I do, each fighting for their own ground? Or was he a hard man, insisting on being master of the house, as most Greek men did? They lived in a paternalistic society where men were, at least in public, undisputed boss —but then again, despite feminist inroads, so do I, to a lesser extent. And did Mary chafe at the bit, wanting room to breathe? I long to know more about her.

Their marriage lasted—ten children and nearly 40 years —but was it passion that held them together, or duty, or simply a lack of an alternative for Mary?

I'd like to think they were each other's lifelong passion.

It's something I think more about as I get older—how relationships, like passions, endure. What keeps them alive? I see Ghikas' marriage through the filter of my own understanding of love and passion over time.

While writing is my new passion, John is—and always has been—my greatest.

Talking about no regrets, it's time for a sweet fix. I try Aunt's *amygdalota*, and, wow, wow, wow. It tastes of heaven and the Elysian Fields, where souls live in immortal bliss for eternity. Do you know that taste?

I read online that some versions are cooked, but this isn't.

The icing sugar has turned hard on the outside, while the inside is soft and slightly chewy. It's traditionally made with blanched almonds, rose water, and semolina—Aunt's addition of a hint of orange blossom water translates into the most heavenly, delicate flavour.

While I'm enjoying it, I search Hydra real estate online. Not quite as bad as Maria thought, and quite a number available. Mental note: Maria exaggerates. We must be related.

Until tomorrow buddies, *sas periméno*, I wait you.

11

TO PALAMIDAS AND BACK

Seagulls wheel above the harbour in lazy circles, mirroring the slow, measured pace of life on Hydra. Yesterday afternoon the rain drove them to settle on the water, bobbing patiently as they waited. Today they're soaring again.

It's a perfect day for a walk—a chance to step away from the research for a moment, as Maria suggested, and give us and Mrs. Adamopoulou a break.

I've finally cracked the code for the meaning of the double-headed eagle at the church—I emailed Maria—another piece of the puzzle falling into place. It's a widely recognised symbol of Orthodoxy (except to me), representing the unity of church and state. It's also the east and west of the Holy Roman Empire: in the East (Constantinople) and in the West (Rome). But the door knocker I saw had only one head—perhaps it was the messenger eagle of Zeus, king of the Greek gods.

I'm loving the pace of this island, at least in winter. It's slow, economical, and deliberate—in stark contrast to our life back at home, which is surprisingly hectic considering we are retired, with many self-imposed tasks and deadlines. There, I've organised the next day's schedule before I go to bed. Here, I'm noticing a shift in myself—a deceleration that gives me space to think and dream.

What I truly enjoy is when the world around me moves slowly, like here on Hydra, while my thoughts can still race at a million miles an hour. That's when I am most alive—when my mind can choose its own speed and get way ahead, even as everything else slows down.

So buddies, what shall we do today? Should we take the ten-kilometre walk to Palamidas? We could wander up through the back of the town, skirt the hills behind the sea, and then walk down into the valley of Vlychos. It's partly the same track the festival parade took. From there, it looks like an easy walk on a dirt track to Palamidas. Why don't we put our brains into neutral and walk?

Let's breathe it all in.

The forecast promises clear skies. Let's leave the umbrella behind.

To navigate the first part of the walk, I switch on the phone's GPS; Hydra's maze of back streets offers little in the way of signage. But as soon as I climb the hill, clouds drift across, and a light drizzle begins. Let's trust the forecast and press on.

As I stroll along, I spot a boxer dog perched on a rooftop, intently watching the street below. Maybe he's waiting for his owner. He seems blissfully unaware of the height or the oddity of his position. "Dogs don't sit on roofs," I say to him, laughing to myself. How did he even get up there? Must be his usual lookout.

Further on, I come across my first Hydriot chickens. They're being herded by a rather dashing but domineering rooster who's crowing out orders and pecking at them to keep them in line. The hens flap and scatter momentarily, only to settle back to resume their scratching at the ground, clucking among themselves about what a bighead he is.

Of course, I'm captivated by the doors—each at its own stage of colour-fade, with a patina powdered by time. Some are marked with fingerprints revealing the original colour; some wear a blotch of combined prints along one side or around the handle. The intense colour at the outer edges fades in the centre to almost white. Each is beautifully unique, each a minor masterpiece.

Above a high stone wall, I catch a brief glimpse of a stone ruin further along. I walk alongside for a distance—which suggests a substantial block of land—with a small spy hole halfway along offering a tantalising view of the sea and houses below. How funny! What makes a builder go to the trouble of adding that? Maybe he thought giving passersby a peek would keep them from scaling the wall. It surely isn't for those inside to see out, is it? Maybe lovers once used it for secret assignations, whispering soft words, touching fingertips or even kissing through the gap. Sigh. Or maybe it was where the cook threw out the old oil.

I've told you about the even grander Ghikas ruin opposite, on the high side of the track, haven't I? The fire left behind an empty husk of faded plaster and exposed stone, windows that once framed the view now staring out like empty eyes, bordered by weathered brickwork and what's left of the stucco. The structure clings stubbornly to the hillside, as if refusing to give in completely as the earth tries to reclaim it. Below, sheep graze lazily in its shadow.

But the ruin on this side is different—a smaller, more intact house, it stands free on the landscape, not built into the hill like the Ghikas mansion. As I reach the end of the wall, the full extent of its three-storey structure is revealed. Though its roof has collapsed, the walls remain mostly intact, with golden sunlight streaming through the crumbling window frames and gaps in the masonry, creating a shifting play of light and shadow inside. It has its own quiet beauty, more modest but no less captivating.

I am admiring the intricate stonework lining the gully below the house when a man comes along the road through the light drizzle towards me, his shoes encased in blue rubbish bags tied with white string.

"Nice galoshes!" I say.

He looks down at his feet with a smile—obviously delighted with his makeshift solution. I eye his walking stick and the shoe bags with envy.

"Where are you from?" he asks.

"I'm Australian."

His smile widens. "I have been to Australia many times. I work on ship. I love it there. I need to go back," he tells me.

Even on a secluded road on Hydra, there's an Australian connection. Before he continues on his way, he shakes my hand warmly. The meeting eases my slight nerves about being alone on the path. There isn't a serial killer lurking after all.

The path ahead becomes more rocky, uneven. I feel every footstep through my ankles, hips, leg muscles, feet. My focus on the scenery almost results in a few nosedives, reminding me to watch where I put my feet.

I pass a small cemetery clinging to the uphill side of the path and, out of curiosity, I wander in. The only dates I can make out are from the late 19th century—impressive, but not quite what I'm after. Any Voulgaris family graves I might have hoped to find would have had their letters long scrubbed away by time and salty sea breezes. I keep walking.

A fisherman overtakes me on the downward path, rod in hand.

"I hope you catch one!" I call out to his retreating back.

Without turning, he waves his rod in acknowledgement and laughs. "Maybe!"

The path merges with the coast at Vlychos, leading onto the dry weather road. I know this because the alternative route takes you over an impossibly high but gracefully arched bridge, likely built for those rare times when the now parched waterway transforms into a raging torrent. It's hard to imagine the kind of rain or flood that would necessitate such a majestic structure. It was built in 1825, during the Greek War of Independence, by a brave French general, Karolos Favieros (Charles Favier), who helped train the Greek troops.

The bridge underwent a renovation about 20 years ago.

A sign points towards a tavern, and I follow the arrow, thinking a cup of coffee would be nice.

No luck. The place is deserted. Many of the houses look like holiday rentals, shutters all closed for the season.

The dirt path hugs the coast, with steep drops to the sea,

and is much gentler on the feet and legs than the stone paths. I pass a farmer throwing fertiliser from a bucket, a timeless action of pellets spraying in wide arcs across grass terraces.

A few sheep graze nearby, uninterested.

That is all.

It is enough.

When I arrive, the inlet at Palamidas is also deserted, with a narrow pebbly beach stretching along the water's edge. Behind a rock wall, boats rest on their sides, waiting for repairs. Two houses nestle against the hill, the barking of an invisible dog the only sign of life, adding to the quiet isolation. There are no indications of the ruined mansions I've heard about, nor any cafés. Maria said there's a Voulgaris 'summer house' here, and the Turkish Kapoudan Pasha, admiral-in-chief of the Ottoman fleet, used to stay there whenever he visited Hydra. He wouldn't have been welcome at the port.

Thirsty yet content with my exploration, I decide not to venture further.

On my way back, I pass a few of the island's 300 churches, most locked up for winter. The tavernas, too, are closed, their doors shut tight against the wind. A horse waits patiently, tied to a fence, perhaps for the farmer I saw scattering fertiliser earlier. As the sun occasionally breaks through the clouds, the sea turns to a sparkling blue green. The little water taxis are still active, zipping along the coast —two seem to be racing each other.

I'm selfishly enjoying the deserted beaches, quiet tavernas, and shuttered churches—but it's also nice to imagine them soon alive with sunbathers and summer crowds. I came here to uncover Ghikas' story, but I'm finding that the real joy is in the experience itself—Klein would approve.

Before I know it, I'm back at Kamini. The old ochre and oxblood coloured building on the marina—where I caught the water taxi the other day—looks even more paint-peeling and neglected. On the coastal track between Kamini and Hydra, there's a memorial seat to Leonard Cohen, offering a brilliant view. I pass another horse, head drooping in the shade, waiting for its owner.

After three and a half hours, my focus is now more on my feet and my stomach than the scenery.

I look for and find the restaurant Manna (turn away from the harbour at the Alpha Bank, Vasso told me), where I order slow-cooked Cretan lamb. Or perhaps it's lamb cooked in the Cretan way. Either way, it's delicious.

Naturally, now that I'm back from my walk, the weather has turned fine. I wander into another shop where the owner tells me that Spoiled doesn't open until the season begins. Of course it doesn't.

Next, I pop in to see Aunty Flora to buy more *amygdalota*. She greets me with that lovely smile that crinkles up her eyes in her quietly warm way. She shares her secret: it lies in *anthonero,* the scented water she makes each year when the bitter oranges are in bloom. And there's no semolina in her mix.

Don't try to analyse it, I tell myself, as I walk home chewing. Just eat the stuff and enjoy it. I pass a yard that could belong to Steptoe and Son, cluttered yet utterly charming. Provided you don't live next door, I guess.

I buy some beautifully ripe tomatoes at a grocery store—far too many for me alone. I drop some off at Eileen's store, where I find Nicoletta. Eileen appears and insists on treating me to a limoncello. Although I'm not a fan of sweet liqueurs, I sip a little. It's yummy.

I spend some time photographing reflections at the water's edge.

Back in the apartment, I think about the timeless simplicity of island life. The closed tavernas and deserted beaches whisper the quieter season—inviting me to slow down and appreciate a farmer scattering fertiliser by hand, horses resting in the shade, boats being repaired.

Usually, when I visit a place, I'm a whirlwind with a checklist—racing around, seeing everything, ticking boxes with a vengeance, desperate about what I've missed. Hydra is slowly soothing the frantic perfectionist out of me.

I don't need to blitz through the whole island in two weeks. As much as I hate to admit it, I'm beginning to see the wisdom in what Klein says about taking life at a slower pace. This journey is becoming more than uncovering history. Can I accept it's about me looking at the world—and my place in it—with fresh eyes?

This slower pace has also made me reflect on my writing. All through my education the system pressured students to write in a certain way, in a 'literary' style. To meet expectations, win awards, or fit the mould of what a 'real writer' should be. But just as the island has encouraged me to slow down and notice the details, it's teaching me that authentic writing comes from being true to myself. It's not about fitting someone else's idea of writing, or about aping anyone else—it's about letting my own voice emerge, naturally and honestly, while I take my time and (hopefully) enjoy the process.

To Palamidas and Back

I hear bed calling. I hope you enjoyed our stroll today, the soft dirt underfoot and watching the farmer at work.

Until tomorrow, buddies, when we visit Mrs. Adamopoulou again—our delightful daily ritual.

And we're having lunch with Maria. *Ti oraía!* That will be fun!

12

I SEE THEM HERE, I SEE THEM THERE

After yesterday's walk on those rough stones, my feet feel as if they've been through an olive crusher. Nothing another trek won't fix.

The apartment coffee maker is a dripolator machine—a device as mysterious as it sounds. My first cup on that first day was so strong it could have put hairs on a baby's chest. Or powered a boat engine. On day two, I accidentally used water from the soda water bottle. Sparkling coffee, anyone?

This morning, though, I nail it. The right brew to prepare me for the next Mrs Adamopoulou raid—I'm on the right frequency. But can I be bothered trying again?

What did you say?

Persistence is king?

Yes, buddy, you are right.

Then another piece of excitement. A woman walks beneath my window with a donkey in tow. I haven't seen a woman donkey handler before—I race downstairs for a photo. Luckily, a truck full of soil is blocking her way

(Another of the two trucks? Are they having babies?), so she hasn't gone far. The sweet donkey, bags folded on her back, is here to carry her own hay home for a takeaway dinner. Her owner, a strong and independent woman, patiently allows me to take a few pictures. Or maybe slightly impatiently.

I dash back upstairs to grab my things for the archives, and by the time I return, she's already loaded the darling donkey with two big bales of hay and is heading home. We greet each other almost like old friends. Then I amble towards the other side of the port, pausing here and there to take photos. I arrive a little after 10am.

Stam is at the front desk with my friend from the other day—it's hard to believe she's the same person. It definitely must have been me.

"Is Mrs Adamopoulou in, Stam?" I ask casually, keeping my tone light and easy.

"Yes, she is," says Stam.

My jaw drops. Slowing down is working. I've entered the new time zone.

"But she's busy on the phone," he adds, as if reminding me not to get too excited.

Ah, thank goodness. Order is restored in the world.

"May I wait?" I ask, settling into the moment, sure she will yet disappear.

"Of course," says Stam.

I wander through the archives again, noticing things I'd overlooked before. Like the Voulgaris mansion doors on display between the first and second floors.

Time passes. More time passes. I am staying. I find an extraordinary book in the gift shop—the entire diary of a real man on board a ship during the Greek War of Independence. In Greek. Pity. I would really love to read that.

Finally, suddenly, she is here.

"I'm sorry to keep you waiting," says Mrs Adamopoulou. She's wearing a deep red sweater and has a warm, approachable smile that puts me at ease, and a subtle confidence. A pair of sunglasses rest on top of her head and large, circular earrings sway as she moves. "Won't you come in?" Her shoulder-length brown hair falls in soft waves.

Inside her office, a tiny Chihuahua in a hand-knitted green jacket greets me from behind the door.

"That's my dog, Miltos," she says with a welcoming smile.

"How gorgeous," I reply, relaxed by her easy charm. The dear little puppy could be a fire-breathing dragon, and I'd still admire it.

We speak for fifteen minutes about my research, and the dead ends we've encountered. She suggests the town hall in Athens and then mentions: 'You know we have a book about the family, don't you?'

I gape. "The one by Papamanolis written in 1930?"

"Yes," she confirms.

"You have it?" I repeat, like an idiot.

Mrs A smiles. "Yes, we have it. I'll have Eleni fetch it for you."

I think, "You little ripper," or something equally erudite.

I don't say that Eleni and I have already searched for it. Instead, I tell her how I've been writing to antique bookstores in Athens over the past six months, searching for a copy.

Fortune favours the bold. 'Mrs Adamopoulou, may I photograph the book? I'll find someone to translate for me."

"Of course you may."

Too easy.

I return to the front desk. "Isn't she wonderful, Stam?" I gush. "Do you know my family thinks you've murdered Mrs Adamopoulou to take her wages."

Stam bursts into hearty laughter. "Yes, yes, yes," he says, "that's exactly what we've done. We've hired an actress!"

This delightfully playful response catches me off guard. I laugh with him.

Upstairs, Eleni is holding the book. I almost dance her around the room. Panagiotis is there too.

"Where was it?" I gasp.

"In the other room," she grins.

She hands it to me with a gentle smile and says, "*The Voulgaris Family of Hydra*".

I hold the yellowing booklet against my chest, wearing a Cheshire cat grin, a musty smell drifting around me. I look at the soft cardboard cover—of course I can't read a single word. It's like being given the key to a treasure chest and discovering it's rusted shut. But I'm over the moon. Ghikas' name may be in these pages.

"Would you like a cup of Greek coffee?" Panagiotis asks.

I have a lot of photographing to do. "Yes, please," I answer, though it never arrives. Nice of him to offer. While I'm taking photos, he is busy deciphering the signatures on the declaration of war in 1821 with a magnifying glass, searching for names from our hero's family. What a darling.

It doesn't take long to photograph the 160-odd pages of the book. By then it's nearly 1pm, and I'm more than ready for lunch with Maria—a glass of wine sounds heavenly.

When I get to Psarapoula, one of the boys opens the door

to say they are closed for a funeral. He seems ok with that. I text Maria.

She's ok too. "OK. Let's go to Piato," she texts back. "Can we make it 1.30?"

Any time is OK. I don't have any other plans. I'll have a wine while I wait.

Katerina is warm in her welcome. "I've made a vegetable soufflé for you," she says.

When Maria arrives, she wants to know what I've found out. As I tell her about the Papamanolis book, I realise that my tentative researcher has given way to a more confident investigator.

But she says, "The Papamanolis book could be written in literary tense—it's difficult to translate." I remember in my French studies, when we learned a formal tense called 'preterite'. Must be the same sort of thing. I'll deal with it somehow.

We both order the soufflé, and Maria orders an ouzo. She fills it with water. We talk non-stop with Katerina tut-tutting, "Your food is getting cold!"

The salad is a mountain of bright greens and juicy tomatoes, topped with enough cucumber and olives and feta to make me Greek. It's far too big for us. Maria is staying in Piraeus with her brother for the weekend so she can't take it home.

Her website should be finished soon—one of his friends is helping her.

"I hope he's yummy," I say. She blushes.

We chatter on about her studies. She asks about my walk to Palamidas yesterday and wants to see my photos.

First the dog on the roof.

"Oh, my goodness," she says. "That dog is Milva Voulgaris."

Imagine my reaction.

"He belongs to Ioannis Voulgaris. Son of Peter Voulgaris. Son of Aunty Flora who made our amygdalota."

The donkey photographs I took—Ioannis Voulgaris is in one of them.

She flicks further, exclaims over each photo, asks if she may have copies.

The lovely ruin belonged to the Kriezis family. No, not the Voulgaris—although Antonis married Uncle Governor Giorgios' daughter. Maria's father rented this land when she was a child, and she and her siblings played all the time in the ruin. She knows it like the back of her hand. Her father's villa is quite close. And I've told you about the ruin on the top side of the road that belonged to Nikos Ghikas, whose lifestyle was in stark contrast to Hydra's other insanely talented artist, Panagiotis Tetsis…

Maria comes to the photo of our blue bag man. She laughs. 'You won't believe this. This man is a Voulgaris too.'

By this time, I am really laughing. "You're making this up!' I chortle.

"No, really!" she says earnestly.

She keeps flicking. Finally, she is up to this morning, and our woman with the donkey. She puts her hand over her mouth, laughing again. 'She lives at Kamini. Her name is Tassia Voulgaris.'

And that pearl-grey cat lounging on the rampart the other afternoon? No, not a Voulgaris—her name is Froufrou, which sounds about right. Speaking of cats, I forgot to mention: Skotádi has moved on. Apparently, he got a better offer—he probably has his own butler.

Maria mentions the Voulgaris 'summer house' ruin at Palamidas that I've missed. I'm kicking myself for letting the threat of the dog stop me.

My wariness stems from an experience a few years ago while I was out walking. I've always believed dogs respect confidence, but I made the mistake of locking eyes with one dozing on the top step of his house. In my brightest voice, I called out, "Hello, old fellow! Enjoying a rest in the shade?"

Well, he gave a deafening bark, leapt off the top step like a rocket, and came barrelling down the path toward me with all the charm of an enraged bear, teeth bared in a ferocious snarl. I braced, fully expecting him to clear the hedge in one furious leap. Thankfully, he stopped short, still barking. I didn't hang around. Since then, I've approached strange dogs with extreme caution. And I never eyeball them.

But now it's cost me the Voulgaris house at Palamidas. Shades of *Mission Impossible*—if only I had Tom Cruise's nerve. Or at least his stun gun. Only kidding.

Lunch with Maria is less like a meal and more like a meeting of minds. It's amazing what you can learn when you're open to new perspectives, when you collaborate, share, and listen more than you speak—I bite my tongue.

After she leaves to take a history class, I linger a little to finish my meal. It's been a productive day: finally tracking down Mrs. Adamopoulou and finding the Voulgaris family book, even if no one can translate it, sharing a meal with Maria, and enjoying Katerina's happy chatter. I don't manage to eat all the salad, so Katerina kindly packs it up for me to take home. With a new boat in the port, the shops are buzzing. I wander past a store, and the shopkeeper—an attractive older woman with a twinkle in her eye—waves me inside.

"Ah, my favourite visitor!" she exclaims. "Come in! I have just the thing for you today."

"Oh, really?" I ask, amused. "What is it?"

She holds up the same evil eye bracelets I've seen everywhere. "Perfect for the little ones, no?"

I laugh. "Alright, you've convinced me." Actually, I've bought all my gifts.

I buy three, one for each of our granddaughters. And a disc for our grandson. That should take care of their futures. As I head back to the apartment, I'm still thinking about the difficulty of translating the Voulgaris book, and the mansion I missed at Palamidas.

I go for a walk to clear my head, and as I wander along the cobblestone street, I pass Commo Gusto—a hairdresser shop slash nail bar. There's a sign in the window saying, "Massages by appointment". I pause, feeling the familiar pull of the schedule I haven't yet worked out for tomorrow—there's much still to do, people to meet, archives to visit. Yet, I want to break away from routine. Why not? What would happen if I did absolutely nothing?

The thought is deliciously rebellious. Not having a plan is wicked. I think of *andante*. I make up my mind. I'm going to waste tomorrow morning. I'm going to book a massage and let myself drift.

When I'm back at the apartment, I google Greek massage to see if they're usually hard or soft. I'm a softie myself. I read these words: "A Greek massage specifically implies the main source of stimuli is spitting on the person's back."

Oh my god.

I search again.

Some Geek masseurs use the Hippocratic method: dry rubbing with powder, horsehair brush on the shoulders, oil massage and then cupping. With fire.

I'm not sure if I'd rather be spat on or burned.

Then the website speaks of the ending: the head massage, otherwise known as the "rubbing of sorrow". It doesn't say whether it gives sorrow or takes it away.

So while they probably can't fix this minor writing crisis, something will happen!

Until tomorrow, buddies, *pánta sas periméno*. I always wait you.

13

SHAMPOOING AND SIMPLICITY

When I open the shutters this morning, the windowpane is fogged, and it's raining as forecast.

But it soon fines up to a blue, blue, day.

Did I tell you I sent Iliana a text a few days ago to ask where I'd find the apartment manual? I haven't been sure where to take my rubbish—I don't want to invade someone else's bin, and there's no sign in any of the cupboards of a list of apartment instructions or contacts.

Iliana is full of apology—she lives in Athens and only comes here for the summer; the last guest lost it; she'll have another printed. I say an emailed pdf will be fine.

This is what arrives in my inbox:

WELCOME TO THE WHITE HOUSE
   WI-FI PASSWORD: xxxx

CLOSEST SUPERMARKET: on your right as leaving the apartment. Super K.

GARBAGE: There is a garbage bin walking on your left leaving the apartment (you can leave the garbage between 7am and 9am)

EMERGENCY CONTACT: xxxx

Enjoy your stay!

I LAUGH out loud when I see it. No wonder the last guest lost it—it was so small! I told you Hydra was economical. Manuals go minimalist—if they ever existed. I love it.

It reminds me of an instruction sheet our daughter Ange and I were once given in Italy: "If the electricity breaks off, it should arrive immediately. If it does not happen, probably there is another damage that will be arranged at once." It also said, "It is forbidden speaking vulgarly especially in the hours of rest."

Iliana's manual, as small and unassuming as it is, gets the job done. I'm always obsessed with nailing every detail, covering all the bases, but I'd be better prioritising simplicity instead. And perhaps my writing doesn't need to be perfect —just honest and clear—the essence without the clutter.

John would certainly approve. He's always been one for cutting through the noise, seeing things simply and clearly in black and white. He hates flowery writing with a passion, preferring words that get straight to the point, whether in what he reads or in what he says. He speaks his mind plainly, without fear or hesitation. That's his secret to aging well: he doesn't overcomplicate things although he's a planner too.

Klein might say that's part of a stoic approach to life—finding contentment in simplicity, seeing things for what they are without all the fuss. Never complaining. That's courage.

It's ironic, really. Maybe that kind of clarity is what landed Ghikas in the trouble he found himself in. Speaking too plainly or refusing to bend might have been his undoing. Then again, maybe if he'd had more of John's simplicity of vision, there wouldn't be a story at all—no mystery, no loose ends. And I wouldn't be here, chasing after fragments of his life.

Speaking of simplicity, despite Iliana's clear and concise manual, I still have no idea where to find the rubbish bin.

My research notes are growing like an olive tree—roots reaching further and further out, branches twisting in every direction. Assassinations, secret societies, powerful men, deadly fire ships, naval battles. I start at one point and before I know where I am, I've followed a trail such a long way that I can't even remember what the original search was about. One thing is certain. You didn't want to make enemies in 19th century Hydra. Is that what happened to Ghikas? He made one enemy too many?

I've had a shower, ready for my *masáz*. I set off a little nervously.

I'm grateful Angelika at Commo Gusto hasn't read the information I found last night. My hour with her is perfect. When I leave, my head is in the clouds without an ache in any of my million muscles.

But when I descend the spiral staircase back down to the shop, a fellow customer notices my wet hair—I've had a shower and shampooed it.

"Oh dear," she says, "It's cold outside. You'll have to cover your head."

It's the most glorious day.

"I went outside with wet hair once," she says, "and I had much pain in my head for months."

The other girls nod in agreement.

I don't have a hat—I promise I'll go home and dry it.

I call in to Sassa. "Your hair is wet," she says. "You must dry it. You'll get sick."

I am beginning to believe them. I risk buying a dress first—the lightest cotton, almost a seersucker, floor-length with splits to the knees. And a shirt for John in the same fabric.

I'll dry it after lunch at Piato. Tony doesn't care about my hair. He brings me felt pens and a plate.

"You draw, I put it on the wall," he says, smiling.

I thank him but put them aside. I'd need a week's planning. "Is there any crime on Hydra?" I ask.

"None," he says. 'A friend of mine asked me last week to go and check his house before the tourist season starts. When I arrived, I found his keys still in the door—they've been there the whole winter."

How beautiful. Trust defines life here.

I say that Piato must be very busy in the season.

Tony says, "Oh yes, people are waiting in long queues for meals. I have seven waiters, and five cooks in the kitchen. It's bedlam. Last year, as I was rushing around, a man asked me if he could use the restaurant for a photo shoot. I said yes and thought no more about it."

"Then in October, a man arrives and says 'OK, I'm ready for the shoot.' 'What shoot?' I ask. 'I asked you in the summer,' he says. 'Oh, OK fine,' I say. Next thing, who turns up? Vivienne Westwood, Pamela Anderson and a heap of models. Can you believe it? Look, here are the photos."

There are lots of Pamela Anderson standing on a table.

Katerina has the most beautiful face. "Make sure you come tomorrow or Monday," she says. "We're going to have *sagros*—it's a lovely fish."

"How does the fisherman know he'll have *sagros*?" I ask.

"He goes to his secret place and uses special bait."

Sounds delicious.

After lunch, I decide it's warrior woman day, the day to tackle the steep climb up the 1500-foot hill to the Monastery of Profitis Ilias—the Prophet Elijah.

Fast forward five hours. I am back now, at 6pm, with the sun kissing the sides of the buildings. I'm lying on the bed, totally bushed.

I'm thinking about Hydra's secrets, held tight by the islanders and only shared with those they trust. I've heard whispers of dark deeds—blood feuds and knifings, massacres during the war on both sides.

Every day, I'm a little more at home here, but Hydra's like an onion, with layer upon layer of secrets. For every layer I peel back, there's another underneath, like an inevitable plot twist at the end of a novel.

Even the fisherman's favourite spot for catching sagros is a secret he keeps to himself. I look it up. Sagros is *diplodus sargus*, a white sea bream prized in Mediterranean cuisine.

I'll tell you about the climb to the monastery tomorrow buddies.

For now, *tha íthela na xekourastó*—I would like to rest.

14

ASCENT TO PROFITIS ILIAS

Let me tell you about the walk up to the Profitis Ilias monastery yesterday afternoon. It's a 500-metre climb, nearly to the island's pinnacle—both literally and historically—featured in every tourist brochure for its stunning views and also its significance during the War of Independence. And for the fact that the town always stationed a lookout somewhere up there, to watch out for attack.

I was planning on an easy day after my morning massage—my hair was finally dry, but my head was still full of dates and facts from the internet and the archives. I decided instead that a hike up a mountain was exactly what I needed to clear my mind. And the weather was spectacular—ideal for a long walk.

As I left the apartment, George from the shop three doors down said, "Where are you going? Off to conquer the world?"

"Up to the monastery," I answered, pointing vertically into the sky, as if I were going on a space mission.

George raised an eyebrow. "Profitis Ilias? That's quite a climb. Do you have an umbrella?" he asked, looking genuinely concerned.

"I don't think I need one, do I? Look at the sky, George!" We both looked up at the glorious blue cloudless expanse.

"Shelley, if you need one, and you don't have one, and it's raining and cold and dark and windy, you'll be sad."

Well, when George put it like that, only a madwoman would go without one.

Actually, only a madwoman would go up there at all in weather like that. Did he say dark? Surely, I'd be back before then! But I loved his concern. George wasn't only being cautious—he was being thoughtful in a quiet way, thinking ahead for me, even in perfect weather. What a beautiful, kind soul. So I dutifully retraced my steps, grabbed an umbrella, and tossed it into my bag—adding what felt like an extra tonne. Thanks, George!

I turned on Google Maps—essential for navigating Hydra's winding streets and avoiding the embarrassment of having George send out a search party if I didn't return. A website says the return hike to the top and back, a climb of 500 metres, takes about two hours (if you've lost your mind) or four hours (for mere mortals). Simple.

I left town on the only street that seems to have a name—Miaoulis. Yes, the one and only admiral. As I climbed, I glanced back at the winding road and spotted a house on the last corner which had stepped straight out of a French Impressionist painting. Once out of town, the path turned to concrete, which quickly morphed into a loose, stony track.

Oh, perfect. A vertical rockslide. My shoes were about as useful as flip-flops. Why didn't I pack my tractor-tire hikers when I had the chance? This, buddies, is how empires crumble.

But it was only a trick. The stony path turned back into washed-out concrete—and then into a proper, crazy-paved pathway with the stones set in concrete, zigzagging up the steep slope. I took my time, stopping to look back and photograph the odd grassy terrace dotted with olive trees, the ruin of a stone house. Occasionally, I heard the gentle tinkle of sheep bells—the delightfully soothing sound I needed, because my feet were throbbing and sweat was pouring off me as if I'd run a marathon.

At this time of year, the island is green, with soft grasses covering the terraces and tinting the rocky hillsides. In the summer photos I've seen, it's a different story—the island is baked to an inhospitable brown, the waterfront so densely packed with sun-bronzed tourists you couldn't slip a cigarette paper between them.

I hope Hydra never slicks itself up for them. I don't think it will.

Lucky me, I've got the quieter, greener Hydra—most of my photos of the harbour and quay are empty of people. Only the metal uprights along the water's edge, with swinging overhead ropes attached to the flat-fronted buildings to support awnings, show that the crowds will arrive in summer. A few small, mismatched shades stick out over the shopfronts, adding a haphazard unpolished charm, the essence of Hydra. It's almost as if Hydriots refuse to make too many accommodations for tourists, except to make sure they keep coming. And that's why they do.

I hadn't seen another soul on the track until a tall, slender young priest in a black cassock appeared, heading towards me. We exchanged smiles, and he shrugged to acknowledge the language barrier before we went our separate ways.

By then, my smile had twisted into a grimace—my sneakers had turned into a medieval form of punishment, with each rock stabbing my soles.

A faded, hand-painted sign claimed I had only half an hour to go. Ha! Who were they kidding?

The path weaved through a shady pine forest, and on the other side I had a glorious view of the harbour and the Peloponnese peninsula—the blue hills of the mainland, the port far below with its tiny houses and ships—everyone going happily about their business, completely unaware of my epic struggle. Except for George and Google. But George knew I had an umbrella, so it was hardly epic.

The proper stone-paved path gave way to rough stones set in the ground, then dry stone steps—both built for function, not speed. The kind of surface that demands you watch your footing.

Up ahead, I spotted a young woman sitting on a low wall, absorbed in her camera, with a black Labrador standing alert beside her.

No need to worry, I told myself. The dog will be friendly.

Using my best "I'm just passing through, nothing to see here" body language I gave him a wide berth without making eye contact. Sophie turned out to have no English and we communicated in my passable French. She was affectionately calling the dog Ébène—Ebony. He had adopted her halfway up the mountain and she had no idea where he'd come from, but at least he was friendly.

She mentioned that there's only one caretaker priest at the monastery now, and he lives in town. Probably the young priest I ran into earlier—the daily climb would explain his lean physique. Anyway, now we saw no one. I took the gentler zigzag path while Sophie and Ebony tackled the steeper, shorter steps. Finally, we both reached the simple, weathered ironwork gates together, featuring a traditional Greek geometric pattern.

As I stood there looking into the walled compound, I thought about how I had read in one of my history books that the church, and this monastery in particular, played a key role in the politics of the Greek Revolution in 1821. The Hydriots once jailed one of their own leaders—Theodoros Kolokotronis—and his son right here, in the monastery, for four months. Tourists can even visit the cell. His crime? It's blamed on his falling out with Giorgios Kountouriotis, Hydra's executive officer during the revolution. It probably didn't help that Kolokotronis was neither navy nor an islander.

It made me wonder, though—where did Nicholaos stand on that? Was he for or against locking up a fellow Greek who was also fighting for freedom? And what about Ghikas? It's the sort of decision that I imagine could cause dissension. Did Ghikas follow his father's lead, or did they fall out over it? Could that have been the beginning of a rift between them? Perhaps they didn't see eye to eye at all.

As we pulled back the bolt and opened the gate, Ebony slipped inside the grounds with us. Sophie and I looked at each other. Oh well. Perhaps he lived here. The place was deserted, but the huge doors into the monastery were ajar, and above the lintel was a lovely gilt mosaic. I think it depicted the horses of fire that took Elijah to heaven. You're right—I looked it up on my phone. ☺

We were unsure if the open door was an invitation, but when Ebony went straight into the vaulted entryway, we followed. The dark room on the left was lined with shelves of desiccated herbs and dusty handmade soaps to sell tourists, along with an antiquated water bubbler that, surprise, surprise, didn't work. On the right-hand wall was a Madonna cradling an almost adolescent Jesus.

Should we go further? Ahead was a quadrangle and the church in the centre, constructed of mid-grey stone highlighted by white-washed mortar. Ebony strolled out, seemingly at home.

Suddenly, from somewhere deep within the monastery, came the most enormous, reverberating barking of a massive, savage dog. Ebony bolted back into the entryway. His wild eyes told me it was Cerberus, the three-headed dog from Greek mythology. I believed him. Sophie was behind me. Honestly, I wasn't sure who was the most frightened of the three of us.

I quickly took a photo of the beautiful church in front of me—proof that I'd made it, in case I didn't make it back down.

In silent agreement, Sophie and I left. Ebony had already retreated.

We wandered around the dear little locked chapel at the end of the grass terrace, with its old gravestones, one with intricate marble carving.

Though I'd reached the monastery, I hadn't seen inside it

Ascent to Profitis Ilias

—just as I've come to Hydra but haven't yet found answers about Ghikas' parents. It felt like standing on the edge of something, close, yet still on the outside looking in.

Did Ghikas ever feel the same? Did he reach his goals, or was he always chasing something just out of reach? I wonder if he ever regretted staying in Australia, far from his birthplace. Or did he eventually make peace with his choices, even the ones that led him into exile?

I decided that next time I'd conquer Mount Eros, another 90 metres higher. But not today. We continued west, down the hill beside the monastery wall, toward the sprawling buildings of the Nunnery of Agia Efpraxia. Founded in 1825 during the revolution. It, too, was deserted. Until recently, the nuns practised their embroidery here—maybe they've escaped for the off-season, too. The tall umbrella pines reminded me of the ones you see in Italy.

Sophie headed back up to the monastery, with Ebony stuck to her like glue. I took the faster route, cutting diagonally from the nunnery. When I rejoined the steps, I spotted Sophie and Ebony still up at the gates. I called out, and Ebony came barrelling down to me like I was his long-lost owner.

I waited for Sophie to catch up and we said goodbye as she and Ebony continued purposefully back to town, while I continued to wander. I noticed dear little blue grape hyacinths in the grass beside the path—I hadn't seen them on the way up, so I knelt for a better view.

That's when another flower caught my eye—one I recognised from my gardening books. A fritillary! A teeny nodding yellow and brown bell of a fellow—and not only one, but a whole battalion of them chattering away with the grape hyacinths. I googled them on the spot. It was *fritillaria rhodokanakis*, a tiny lily—and an endangered species found only on the island of Hydra and neighbouring islands.

I was as thrilled as if I'd discovered the lost city of Atlantis. But don't worry. I kept my enthusiasm dignified. More or less.

Way down below I could see Sophie with Ebony still by her side—they were almost back in the town, turning the S-bend. Maybe Ebony lived in town?

It goes to show. If I'd gone with them, I wouldn't have found those little treasures.

It was getting late by this time, and I had the mountain all to myself. I put my bag on a stone step, rough, uneven, but solid, and sat on it, hands around my knees like I was seven again. The wind had picked up, and when the sun occasionally broke through the racing winter clouds, the warmth felt sweet.

I found myself smiling at the absurdity of it all—71, alone on a mountain in the freezing wind of a Greek winter, chasing a pirate. But what fun.

I wonder what Ghikas would make of it. I think he'd be blunt. "Do you have the guts to finish this, girl?"

The climb was a slog, no way around it—complete with a "why the hell am I doing this?" moment halfway up. But if I'd stepped out of my door and been handed that view on a silver platter, it wouldn't have meant anything. The effort is what gave it value. Same with Ghikas. I came here expecting to find neat, tidy answers about who he was. That didn't happen. But the chase? That's what hooked me. The archives, the dead ends, the conversations, the questions spinning in my head—it was all part of the thrill. I didn't need the full story tied up in a bow—good thing, since my talent for not finding answers has been nothing short of spectacular. But that won't stop me from digging. Not now. Not ever.

Turns out, the joy is in the chase, not the prize. How often have we heard that before?

We're all chasing something, aren't we? Whatever the interest—quilting, planting a new garden, learning a language, picking up painting again, or even starting a whole new career. The beauty is in the work itself—the hands-on effort it takes to create something meaningful. The trick is figuring out what's worth making. And the only way to figure it out? Say yes. Even if it means people give you that look—the one that says, "Is she okay? Should we ring someone?"

But pushing past what is normal 'for my age', or wise—or sane—is how I like to operate. Whether redesigning my garden for the umpteenth time, becoming obsessed with a 200-year-old pirate, or choosing to visit Hydra—a summer resort—in the dead of winter, I've never been one to stick to the script. Setting my own boundaries is the fun part.

But the real jackpot has been my re-invention.

Discovering I can cross out 'cattle farmer', 'gardener', and 'garden designer' from my resumé, and insert 'writer' instead, has been exhilarating—like finding a whole new version of myself I've had locked in a garret. Now, I wake up itching to write and even forgetting to eat. I've found my new obsession, and you'd have to pry the pen from my ink-stained fingers to get me to stop.

As I sit here on this hill, I realise with certainty for the first time, that I *need* to write this novel. Forget my doubts about being a writer, or who can tell this story. With my interest, my research, and my determination to do it, I'm uniquely positioned. Not just for myself, but for Hydra, for Ghikas' descendants, for all Greek Australians, and for Ghikas himself. His story isn't just history—it's a small but important part of Australia's past—his life, from son of a Hydriot shipowner to Australian grazier, was an extraordinary journey. And I'm the one who can bring him back into the light.

Who knows, I might write ten more books, but this one must come first. I've loved reading Klein's insightful observations about aging, and the island, suggesting old age can be a time for reflection and appreciating the fruits of our efforts. Yet while he muses on slowing down, he's also gallivanting off to Hydra. I like his attitude! I'm all about new adventures too—and this book will be one of them. Old age is sharpening my focus because I know I don't have endless time. If my health holds out, others can enjoy the fruits of my labours after I'm gone. If I don't finish, so be it. but I'll give it everything I've got while I can.

I'm lucky to still have the health to climb mountains, both literally and metaphorically, but I also know I need to keep moving to stay that way.

I've loved sharing this trip with you—describing it for you each night in this travelogue has helped me to make sense of what I've seen and read, a way of closing the loop each night. I didn't have to—there's no travelogue police—but I wanted to. And I hope, dear buddies, you've enjoyed travelling with me. I've taken you up a few more stairs than you (or I) probably wanted to climb, and I've been glad of your company. Sure, I could have roped in a friend to come with me—but when I'm chasing a dream, you were the only choice!

John's been part of this too—full credit to him for never clipping my wings (or asking why I want so many feathers). He's always let me chase my dreams, even when they take me halfway around the world.

And let's not forget books—they are the rocket fuel for dreams. They deserve their own bouquet. Even a whole garden.

With the sun sinking towards the horizon, time to head home.

I ease myself off the step, joints protesting the cold, and begin my descent. By this time, my head is like an ice block. I remember the woman in Commo Gusto—I will have pain in my head for months! I fish a scarf from my bag and wind it around my head and throat, in case.

I'm not rushing. I stroll back down, soaking up the view at each turn, with the wind trying to blow me off the path. I am glad to be descending, but I'm not going to cut the experience short. Soon, I am passing the more familiar watsonias and daisies on the edge of town. And just in time, too, as the last rays of the sun light the sides of the houses. George's brolly not needed. But appreciated.

By 6pm, my feet are happy to be back in our warm little apartment, quietly triumphant that Warrior Woman has made it, in more ways than one.

And buddies, this is just the beginning.

15

A DAY OF SMALL DELIGHTS

Since yesterday afternoon's walk to the monastery, I'm pretty sure my left ankle's grown an extra set of bones overnight. Angelika would know what to do. I'm lying in bed, listening to the church bells ringing as they have for centuries. That beautiful clear pure sound feels reassuring: everything is as it should be.

Isn't it funny how each place in the world has its own sound? Something that stays with you long after you've left. You know the feeling—the moment you hear it again, you're instantly back there. I'll bet you've got your own soundtrack too, one that takes you back in time the moment you hear it.

For me, it's the noisy birds at home: the kookaburras' absurd forced laughter, magpies gargling marbles, and black cockatoos screeching in formation overhead.

In Morocco, Turkey, and Iran, the call to prayer enchanted me—amplified through microphones at the tops of the minarets. They were particularly captivating in Istanbul; with such a huge number of mosques, the slightly staggered calls seeming to echo each other. In Cape Town, it was the Noon Gun fired at midday from Signal Hill. In Venice, the gentle splash of water in the canals, lapping softly against the buildings. In India, the streets buzz with car horns, voices, vendors, and the constant hum of daily life. The foghorns in San Francisco. Cicadas in summer in Australia—they have them here too.

Sometimes, sound outlasts place—there's that sound you can't quite identify, but it sticks with you. Somewhere once —can't remember where—a midday siren blared every day to signal it was time to down tools and have lunch. Funny thing is, I still feel the urge to obey whenever I hear a similar sound—though I can't even recall where I was.

I've opened the shutters, and I must tell you, it's a truly pooey day. Rainy, cold, utterly miserable—definitely not the "walk to Mandraki" weather I'd planned. Tomorrow maybe.

I decide to rest and write a little while I try to coax my brain out of its fog. The soothsayers were right. After my hike on the mountain, I have a light head cold—but thankfully not a head full of pain! Ah well, I can't say I wasn't warned.

Speaking of brain fog—though I wasn't—remember the Voulgaris summer house I missed at Palamidas? Well, I didn't tell you there's an olive grove nearby, nestled in a flat-bottomed valley surrounded by gentle hills. It's Hydra's star performer, with olives harvested in the late autumn months of October and November, then shipped off to Ermioni across the channel for pressing. The oil always comes back, but I wonder if some of the trees date from Ghikas' day. Maybe he worked in those groves during the winter months —when the seas were too rough to sail. In those quieter times, men who usually lived by the sea turned to the land, repairing ships or tending the olive groves for food and income.

Well, that's another reason to return. And when I do, I'd love to walk further—it's another hour to Episkopi, where there's more farming land and an old settlement. I'd need hiking boots this time, and a packed picnic—and a guide. Maria!

So now the big question is: where to have lunch? That kind of existential crisis, I'm fully equipped to handle.

After a few hours at the computer, it stops raining. I wander around to Isalos, which is over on the touristy side of the harbour (well, close to the ferry landing and the archives). Isalos always looks busy—the outdoor seating is often full. Because it's busy today too, I sit inside and study the menu—mostly pizza and wraps. The name Isalos means the line where the hull of a ship meets the water. What a beautiful word. But I'm not in the mood for fast food.

As I head back around the harbour, a Greek priest approaches. I ask if I might take his photo. He smiles and points to the departing ferry—ah, timing is everything. I hastily snap a picture. That reminds me—I went to visit George (from the archives) the other day, but his church was closed.

The temperature is about twelve degrees, and it's drizzling again, confusing everyone—one man is hugging himself under his umbrella, bundled up as if it's the Arctic; another man jogs by in shorts.

I stop at Oraia Hydra (meaning beautiful Hydra) on the corner for a proper meal. It opened in 2016 with chef Kosmas Savriadi, who's known for his passion for pure flavours, and sourcing the best ingredients from all over Greece. Eating here feels like the perfect pause before our last day on the island.

I choose two dishes from the mezze menu: taramasalata, which I've never tried before, and fried haloumi—my daughter cooks that for her girls. Tarama is smoked and cured cod's roe, whipped into a dip with lime and soaked bread. A salty, fishy, tangy delight. Kosmas brings out warm home-cooked bread, olive oil and olives. This Greek bread is heavy, dense and golden. Delicious.

I wonder if Ghikas enjoyed something similar in his day. It's an ancient dish, after all—one that ships captains and sailors might have eaten on board, perhaps with lemon juice rather than lime. Did he dip his bread into olive oil as I am?

Tomorrow is our final day on Hydra, and as much as I try to soak in every moment, the reality weighs on me. It's hard to believe it's almost over. I think about how much I've done, and yet there's still much more I could explore. The archives have been fascinating, the walks beautiful, but the feeling of unfinished business is hard to shake. I've uncovered bits of Ghikas' story, but not everything.

Much, much later, the haloumi finally turns up. Kosmas explains his waiter hasn't shown, leaving him to juggle cooking and serving. He's clearly flustered, I feel relieved for him when his fiancée arrives to help. I don't mind the slow service at all, and neither do the other diners—it's wet and cold outside, anyway. What else are we going to do?

Kosmas steps outside into the drizzle for a smoke—it's still common here. I follow him out to ask the identity of the priest in the photo.

A Day of Small Delights

"That's Pater Ionekios from the church of St Demetrios," he says. Suddenly he points and calls out, "Look!"

Three donkeys have escaped and are wandering along the deserted harbour front, neck bells ringing. They look for all the world as if they are out on a casual Sunday jaunt and know exactly where they're going. I almost expect to see them stop for a coffee. Still, if you're trying to make a getaway, the harbour isn't your best bet—they'd have been smarter heading for the hills. I hope they aren't in too much trouble when their owner catches up with them.

On the way home, I buy an ice cream from Netta. It's a foreign concept to me, this idea of doing nothing when I'm travelling, but today I'm enjoying letting the world drift by without rushing to keep up. That fritillary was a quiet delight, wasn't it—a reminder that sometimes, the best things appear when you're not even looking for them. The funny donkeys too.

At dusk, the soft patter of rain taps against the window, and a stray cat tiptoes across a rooftop at the end of the quay. One of the terracotta tiles is darker, an odd patch of shadow. I sit to write, but instead of my meticulously crafted plan, I throw the rulebook out the window. Well not literally. But why not let my writing go where it pleases, like those donkeys? It's liberating—like opening a door and letting the wind rush in.

Writing has become as essential to me as my morning coffee.

There was a time when I poured this kind of energy into my garden—turning the soil, planting, watching things grow. I designed pathways, built pergolas, chose plants that harmonised with each other. But writing is different, messier, more alive. It satisfies me in ways that are freer, with no need for neat lines or boundaries—and thankfully with fewer weeds.

When I was a young woman living out in the bush in rural Queensland—'just a farmer's wife', as they say—I had a lightbulb moment. The farm's fences didn't have to confine me, nor the 25km to town, nor even the 250km to the capital city. I gave myself permission to think bigger.

It started with my garden: when I wanted to know about plants or garden design, I turned to books from all over the world. And the next step was travel. Why not see the world's finest gardens? My children were safe at boarding school and John had no intention of leaving the farm. Off I went—with my garden books, an oversized hat, and a list of gardens to see.

But the truth is, in a caring relationship, pursuing personal dreams requires mutual support. John not only gave his blessing—but more importantly, he made sure the cattle stayed out of the garden while I was away!

His approach to life has always been different from mine. He's always been content with structure and the discipline of boundaries. He thrives on knowing the rules and sticking to them. I love the wonderful strength and security of that. He's my rock—steady, dependable, never needing to chase more. If there's a storm on the horizon, you'll find John out there securing the fences while I'm still inside, wrestling with my raincoat and calculating exactly which way is north. And if John ever changes course, you'll get plenty of notice. There's peace in his predictability, a stability that grounds me.

I'm the opposite. I am a certified rule-bender. I'll spend a week meticulously planning something, then toss it out at the last minute because, *what if?* You hand John a set of instructions, and he'll follow them. Hand them to me, and my first instinct will be to ask, "Why?" When John sees walls, he sees order and safety. I see something begging to be scaled—not in a brave, physical way, mind you—if there's real danger, don't worry, John will go first. I'll be the one bringing up the rear.

Ghikas and Mary—did they balance each other out the way John and I do? Ghikas, with his bold decision to turn to piracy—was that his way of escaping the boundaries his father set for him, a way to claim his own freedom? Or did he act his father's blessing? And Mary, was she content with her world, or maybe resigned to it? Or was there a part of Mary that longed for something more? Did she, like me, question the role she was meant to play and push back against it?

And speaking of remarkable women, let's talk about Laskarina Bouboulina. Now there's someone who didn't wait around for permission. Born in 1771 to a Hydriot father and blessed after his death with a stepfather who admired Catherine the Great of Russia, she shattered every expectation placed on women of her time. After two of her husbands were lost at sea, she took control of her own fleet, financing and commanding ships during the War of Independence. Her flagship, the *Agamemnon*, was the largest in the Greek fleet, bigger than the Ottomans allowed, and she stood on the bridge directing operations in naval battles, at the heart of the action. She's even thought to be the first woman in history to attain the rank of admiral.

But it wasn't only her leadership that made her stand out —it was her refusal to be boxed in. She wasn't content to be a quiet widow, a silent figure behind the men. And yet, her end was as dramatic as her life. In 1825, she was shot dead when her son eloped with the daughter of another local family—a tragic end to a life lived entirely on her own terms.

Perhaps Mary had some of that spirit too. I like to think so.

And speaking of living on our own terms, the forecast for tomorrow promises early rain and then sunshine. Fingers crossed for a perfect blue-sky day, because it's our last one on Hydra, buddies, and as much as I've soaked up every moment, I'm not ready to leave.

Not yet.

So keep your chin up. *Den telíose akóma*. This trip's not over yet.

16

LAST DAY ON HYDRA

The forecast says the rain will stop by 10am, and it does, right on cue. A strong wind blows the last stubborn drops away, clearing the sky for what is our last day on Hydra. It's a bittersweet thought. I'm not ready to leave, are you? Hydra has a way of getting under your skin.

But this is no time for melancholy—this is our last chance to visit Mandraki Bay—a couple of kilometres east of the port. And if I've learned anything, it's that you must make the most of every moment. There's also that photo I've been itching to recreate—one I saw online, showing the town from a stunning viewpoint above. That's the shot I need for my Insta, or, who knows, maybe a future book.

I've found a hike online that looks like it will take us straight to the very spot, and on our last day, it seems as if a hike is written in the stars, don't you think? Is this the last time I'll visit Hydra? Maybe, maybe not. Either way, today's about soaking it all up and capturing that final photo to take a little piece of Hydra with me.

I drop by the archives on the way to say goodbye to Eleni and to exchange email addresses. Although I'll have to come back later because I've forgotten to bring the almond crunch I bought as a gift to thank them.

"I'll contact you if I find anything," she says, and we hug.

And with that, I set off.

All along the steep coastline, steps zigzag down to the water's edge, with concrete aprons for sun-bathing at the waterline. I can almost hear the laughter from summer days, echoing up the cliffs. But today, it's me, a solo hiker.

There's something special about travelling solo. The freedom to follow my own rhythm is one of the greatest rewards. I can walk at my own pace, linger if I like without needing to accommodate anyone else's plans. There are no compromises, no shared itineraries. The island has become my own quiet space for reflection, unbroken by the chatter or concerns of others. I answer only to myself, which means I can sit in silence, change plans on a whim—I hope you haven't minded—or simply soak up the stillness.

The solitude has brought a deeper kind of focus, too—my thoughts are clearer, and the reflections on Ghikas, on why I am here, come without distraction. I can take in everything uninterrupted——a privilege unique to travelling alone.

I discover the most extraordinary little church, wedged between cliffs in a hairpin bend, set in a tiny, picturesque inlet, its whitewashed walls practically glowing against the stone.

As I reach Mandraki Bay, the landscape shifts. The low,

barren hills surrounding the wide bay contrast with Hydra town's steep, dramatic bluffs. I recall reading that Mandraki Bay was Hydra's primary naval base during the 1821 Revolution, and I squint to see the remains of a fort on the opposite headland.

I can't see much else from here—a taverna and resort on the site of the old dockyard, closed, of course, and some bathing boxes on the beach at the far end. If the desalination plant is here, it's well disguised.

Eager to start the hike, I turn back. Earlier, I spotted a steep set of concrete steps climbing the bare-looking rocky hill from the main coastal path, and I'm confident this will take us up the back route over the mountain to Hydra. I hear you asking what can go wrong? I'm laughing. Relax!

I find them again and there's the reassuring yellow and black hiker's mark on a stone seat halfway up. So far, so good. Or does yellow and black mean danger? Oh well. I'm already sweating. I peel off my down jacket and tie it around my waist.

At the top of the steps, a rough boggy bush track leads further up the hill. I've heard Hydra's wildflowers are spectacular in the spring—I'd love to see them. They'd distract me from the gorse scratching my shins, though the knee-high scrub at least gives a clear view over the landscape. Water trickles down the slope, reminding me of last night's rain, and when the track veers left, I wonder if I'm heading away from Hydra altogether. I keep checking that the crest is getting closer, praying it doesn't reveal yet another climb.

Finally, I reach a road. The wind off the sea is sharp and biting, making me struggle back into my jacket. Away a few hundred yards to my left is the Agios Triados Monastery, tempting me with its solitude. I consider a visit, but knowing I still have a couple of kilometres back to town, and suspecting it will be closed anyway, I turn right.

The good road soon peters out—I press on, picking my way over ankle-snapping rocks in the high headwind, trying to remember if I have life insurance. I was expecting to have all these deep thoughts on my last hike—perhaps a last revelation about Ghikas, or a profound moment of insight—but mostly, I'm thinking about whether I'll break a bone. So much for philosophical musings.

The mountains on my left rise higher, the island's spine forming a jagged backdrop.

Our reward? A gorgeous little church on top of the ridge, big enough for two. The gate, secured with a simple clip, swings open easily. Tiny, delicately coloured pastel stones form a small mosaic cross above the door in modern colours: pale pink and chartreuse on a pale blue background. Two graves, or maybe memorials, lie in the churchyard—who were they, I wonder? I forgot to ask Maria about any Voulgaris graves.

As I take photos of a brilliant rosemary bush, an orange butterfly lands right in front of me, a moment of surreal complementary colour harmony.

Places like this show up when we wander off the beaten path, don't they? This whole trip has been like that, hasn't it—stumbling into little moments of clarity and inspiration where we least expect them. Maybe that's the secret: not only to writing, but to life itself. Exploring the unknown and trusting we'll find something worthwhile, even if it's not what we were looking for.

Refreshed by the short stop, I continue walking.

Ahead, across a deep valley, I see the Profitis Ilias Monastery perched on the distant mountain. Aha, civilisation, within reach!

Then, out of nowhere, a waist-high stone wall appears, a barrier running along the top of a cliff. Did I mention I sometimes get vertigo? I inch closer, and the sheer drop on the other side sucks the breath right out of me, as the wind actually pushes me backward. But this is the view I was looking for! It's even more stunning: the whole town spread out below with houses spilling towards the harbour, the harbour itself, the sea stretching out behind it all, Dokos, the mainland beyond, and that magnificent blue sky.

I haven't thought about Ghikas today, but suddenly, I just know he stood here—right here, looking out at this exact view.

And then, in a strange rush, it's not me standing here.

I am Ghikas Voulgaris, the wind blowing my hair across my face, salt on my lips, skin peeling on my ruddy cheeks. Down there is Hydra—my Hydra.

On the opposite ridge, eight-bladed windmills slice the sky like silent watchmen, and a line of donkeys trudges up the hillside, laden with bagged wheat to be ground into flour for the town's bread.

I see my father below in our courtyard, booming out in his heavy voice about politics and war. Always politics and war. And his high expectations of me.

I can almost smell my favourite dish, my mother's stifado, slow-cooked and rich, tempting me back to the family table. My brothers and sisters are already there, elbowing each other as they eat.

The Herakles lies at anchor, ready to sail—now that's where I truly come alive, on the deck of a ship, spray flying in my face, wooden planks creaking underfoot. My friends are waiting at the taverna, calling for me to join them.

This is my Hydra—the sea, the hills, the air.

And yet, somehow, it's too small for me.

Am I a rogue pirate, a patriot—or both?

If I keep standing here in this wind, I'll end up ruddy myself. "Ruddy"—such an old-fashioned word, but that's how the English records described Ghikas' complexion when he landed in Australia. His wasn't just a tan, though; after years of salt spray and sun, his skin would've been tough, burnished. And if he still looked ruddy at 22, even after two years in jail, that weathering must have been permanent.

Standing here on this cliff, I see sheep in the distance. Ghikas did end up a sheep farmer, after all—just like his great-great-grandson, a cattle farmer. Was he, perhaps, more at home on land than sea?

I look up at the jet trails in the sky, then down at the iPhone in my hand. The contrast couldn't be sharper. I can capture this view in pixels and, when I'm at home again, evoke Hydra it in full colour just by looking at the screen in my hand. If Ghikas wanted to see this scene again, he had to piece it together in his mind, rebuilding it from memory and longing.

I take several 'aerial' photos—better than any I've seen online, if I say so myself. I give myself a mental pat on the back for choosing this hike on such a spectacular day. And for my good luck.

I turn right and follow the path down beside a stone wall toward the sea. But where the wall suddenly ends, the path narrows into a steep, shaley ditch, then twists sharply out of sight around a steep bend. A terrifying drop opens up below.

I mutter, "You can do this."

I choose where to place my feet, and with every step, rocks slither under my feet and the wind buffets me.

Panic sets in as I realise I'm a couple of hundred feet up, with nothing but air between me and the town. Fighting a rising tide of terror, I remind myself I can always turn back. I put my head down and focus on my feet, stepping carefully, one foot after another. Each step is a victory. Occasionally, careful to keep my balance on the gravel, I lower myself to a sitting position. Then, with either hand flat on the ground beside me, I lift my eyes to take in the dizzying view.

I tell myself I'm enjoying the scenery and definitely not contemplating my death.

If you ever do this hike, you probably won't recognise it from my description—it's probably a pleasant stroll for most people. But you've been seeing it through the eyes of a world-class scaredy-cat with a PhD in exaggeration.

I meet a man on a donkey coming up the hill. Hydra's donkeys are local heroes, carrying heavy loads, from furniture to building supplies, up and down the steep paths. Sometimes, their handlers ride them back down, which always makes me want to push them off. Today, though, the man looks cheerful. Maybe he's had a tough day. I decide he can stay on.

As I walk down the gentle slope on the paved road back into town, Ghikas is on my mind again. I'm torn between frustration and satisfaction. I still don't know for sure who his father was, though my gut tells me he was the son of *the* Nicholaos from the famous Voulgaris family. I have the photos from the archives, and maybe—just maybe—they'll reveal something, though I'm not holding my breath. If there were anything definitive, Gilchrist would have mentioned it.

But I've walked the same streets Ghikas once did, watched the fishing boats come and go, and seen people going about their lives as they might have in his day. I've stood before houses that have witnessed the same history he lived through. In those moments, I have felt a connection to him—a sense that, in some small way, I've touched the world he knew.

So have my glitzy sneakers—they've certainly earned their stripes, taken all the punishment I've handed out—down hillsides, across slippery flagstones, up stone steps, through the mud. And managed to keep their sparkle through it all.

Before I know it, my twinkle toes are out of the wind in Piato, and I'm greeted by Katerina and Tony's warm smiles. "We have sagros for you."

At that point, I'm more interested in a glass of water.

Katerina sits with me while it cooks, sharing stories of her remarkable life. She and her husband were married when she was fifteen—and they've been married for seventy years—living in Turkey, South Africa and now Greece. Her husband, ninety-seven years old, lives in Athens while she helps her son Tony.

The fish is divine.

"I am going to miss you very much when you go," she says, tears welling up in her eyes.

I put my hand over hers. What a darling.

"Everyone is going to miss you," she continues.

Oh dear, now she's making me cry.

"You are like family,' she adds. "You must come back, and bring your husband, and your children."

"Go on," I say, "You won't even remember me!" And I know she won't. This is simply one of those magic moments.

As Katerina pulls me into a warm hug, I realise how much this place has come to mean to me. Hydra isn't just a backdrop for my story—it's become a part of me, like the people I've met here. I hug her back with a wave of gratitude. Hydra has given me much more than I expected.

Tony breaks us up with practical advice. "This wind will drop by tomorrow. It should be calmer in the morning for the ferry to Athens. You'll be on the 7am?"

I nod. I hope he's right. Sometimes ferries are cancelled in high winds—another reason I have scheduled a buffer day in Athens. I'd rather not miss the flight home.

"I'll have to leave the apartment in the dark," I say, realising I still need to clean out the refrigerator, and pack.

As I stroll home, sea spray leaps above the sea wall, whipped up by the wild wind. I watch a couple of little water taxis struggling against the chop to make it back into the harbour, much as I am struggling to say goodbye to Hydra. But they zoom inside like the little champions they are, into their safe mooring. These two weeks have given me a new sense of purpose—I'm not just going home with notes—I'm returning as an aspiring novelist.

I hear the whisper of the Greek Chorus on the waves, almost as if the island is speaking to me: *"She stood in the shadow of a pirate, yet she found the outline of her own".*

After I finish packing, I set the alarm for 5am—giving me plenty of time for a shower and a leisurely coffee—or two. And enough time to take the rubbish out, pack any last-minute items and haul my suitcase around the harbour to the ferry.

Then I take the thank-you box of almond crunch I forgot this morning around to the archives—what will we do without our daily visits?

You won't believe what Eleni says as I'm leaving.

You will NOT believe it.

"Shelley, I wait you."

"Excuse me, Eleni, what did you say?"

"Shelley, I wait you."

Extraordinary.

I wait you too.

17

A PIECE OF MY HEART

I wake from a dream about folding blankets. As if I'm leaving somewhere. A sudden, sharp thought pierces the fog of sleep. I grab my phone from the bedside.

6.30am! The ferry leaves in 30 minutes.

I almost fall out of bed and dash into the shower. Shampoo, towel off, dress. Where are my sneakers—under the desk. I throw everything into my case—hair still dripping (oh god, months of pain), suitcase half-zipped, toothbrush in hand. Forget coffee. I tie up the rubbish and race out the door.

I fly across the flagstones, suitcase rattling behind me, puffing as if I've been chasing donkeys uphill. How did I sleep through the alarm? Or did I turn it off? Then I remember: I was wide awake at 2am, scribbling ideas for Ghikas' story. Like the old days.

As I round the quay I spot the ferry gliding into the harbour. A sprint to the finish.

I dump my bags and rush into the Cool Mule to return the keys as per Iliana's emailed instruction.

When I come back out, Tony from Piato grins. "Glad you made it. Hope we don't break down."

Break down? I glance at the praying mantis shape of the ferry.

Tony shrugs. "They bought them second-hand from the Russians, years ago."

The ferry is tying up at the dock. As I catch my breath, I glance towards the archives. They're a treasure trove, thanks to Antonios Lignos, Hydra's longtime mayor, who spent decades preserving 18,000 documents. The current team—Mrs. Adamopoulou, Eleni, Stam, Panagiotis, the other Eleni—have shown me such generosity and been more than willing to help. They've made my search not only possible but truly enjoyable. Absolute champions. I can't thank them enough.

And Maria, Katerina, Eileen, the shopkeepers and restauranteurs, George, Ilias, Aunty Flora—each one. I thank them all.

Safely on board, I watch the town as the ferry backs out of the harbour and Hydra recedes in the grey dawn. I press my nose against the glass, watching the island shrink, a mist blurring the familiar shapes of houses and hills.

A piece of my heart is back there on the dock, waving goodbye. As I take one last photo, I whisper, like dialogue out of a corny romance movie, "Don't worry, heart. I'll come back for you." I smile at my own melodrama, but it feels true.

Just as I let out a sigh, my phone buzzes. Probably a reminder that the ferry is leaving.

But no—it's a text from Maria.

"I think you should try contacting this genealogical association in Athens," she says. "They might know more about Ghikas."

A flutter in my stomach. When I thought I was leaving with nothing but beautiful memories and questions! You little ripper, Maria.

I blink. There, on the screen, below the text, is the tiny two-headed eagle—the emblem of the association. My emblem.

The sea becomes choppy as we turn and pick up speed. Hydra disappears behind us, but now my mind's too busy to notice. Two weeks of scouring the archives, chasing down every lead on Ghikas, and now—as I'm leaving—this new clue drops into my lap. Could this be it? The key to finally unlocking his story?

At the dock in Athens, I'm greeted by the usual port chaos—taxis honking, drivers shouting. I've only got one goal: the genealogical association. My taxi drops me at a drab office building. Inside, a caretaker sits behind a glass partition, the gatekeeper of mysteries. I show him the logo. He shakes his head sadly, muttering something in Greek.

Then, "Ahhh, not here."

"Not here? You mean they've moved?" I feel a flicker of panic.

He shrugs, looking as forlorn as I feel. "Né." That means yes. Yes, they're just not here at the moment? Or yes, they've moved?

I stand there like a complete dope. *Research is never a straight line—it's a maze, full of dead ends.* The caretaker gives me a small, sympathetic smile, like he's been through the same battle. I'm tempted to bang my head on his glass cubicle.

Two men in suits enter the building, and the caretaker springs into action.

After a rapid exchange, one of them turns to me. "The association is on the seventh floor, but it isn't open today. Ioannis will give you a phone number."

I nearly hug him but instead, I muster my best Greek accent. "*Sas efcharistó pára polý.*" I hope it means "thank you very much" and not something ridiculous like "does your cat wear pyjamas."

His broad smile doesn't tell me which it is.

Ioannis scribbles two numbers down on a piece of paper. I thank him, forcing a smile. Inside, excitement is trying to choke hopelessness.

I go to a quiet corner to make the calls. I feel slightly sick. Ioannis is watching now, clearly invested. My heart is hammering as the first number rings and rings. With no answer.

The second number—my last chance—rings. Once. Twice. It keeps ringing, while I stare out through the doors at the traffic, the distance between Ghikas and me growing wider with every second.

Ioannis looks equally downcast. I ask for a photo, and he straightens up, putting on his best official expression. It's one of my favourites.

I eat lunch in a café in the CBD. Red roses, starched white linen and a porcini and truffle risotto. I try the numbers again—still nothing.

Back at the hotel I meet Sotiris from This Is Athens, a volunteer guide who's going to show me around the city. I booked this tour back at home before I decided to write a novel, expecting a leisurely wander through Athens. But now, I need to squeeze every bit of historical insight I can from it—I'm on a mission for writing setting, and details that will bring Ghikas' world to life.

"You must be Shelley," he says warmly with a delightful old-world charm, handing me a little hardcover book, *The Companion Guide to the Greek Islands*. Published in 1963. What a beautiful gesture. "A little something to help with your research."

Corduroy blazer and tie, well-pressed jeans. And the kind of manners you rarely see any longer.

But my mind is still on those unanswered calls. I glance at my phone as we head out, half-expecting a notification, a missed call, anything to signal a breakthrough.

Sotiris shares fascinating titbits—at the time of the revolution, Hydra's population was ten times that of Athens. We pass the Zeus temple and I remember the school lessons on the types of columns: Doric, Ionic, Corinthian.

I'm still distracted.

We go past the parliament, the Panathenaic Stadium, and the amazing Acropolis Museum at the base of the Acropolis itself. My mind snaps back to the present. The design by Bernard Tschumi is fascinating: the top floor twists on the footprint of the first and second floors to reproduce an exact copy of the Parthenon's floor plan, with the same orientation.

I'm captivated—by the way the light pours in, the texture of the concrete panels, smooth marble, soaring glass, the full-building width of the steps, the spaces, the voids. Glass panels in the floors for viewing digs.

Sotiris notices. "I think you like the museum's architecture more than the exhibits."

Over coffee on the soaring outdoor terrace, Sotiris talks about the Elgin Marbles like a personal wound. "Byron called it vandalism," he sighs, and I agree. Sotiris is a widower, with children and grandchildren. He loves showing visitors his city.

Normally, this talk would fascinate me. But my fingers are hovering over the redial button on my phone. How close am I to unlocking Ghikas' story?

"You seem worried," Sotiris says with a sympathetic smile. He's just expressed his own outrage that the waiter asked for a tip.

"No. Only chasing ghosts," I reply, smiling.

As we resume our walk around the base of the acropolis, children run to catch soap bubbles. What fun!

"Here we have the Odeon of Herodes Atticus," Sotiris says, pointing to the impressive arched façade of the ancient open-air amphitheatre, the tiers stacked almost vertically. "I've been to many performances here, from Beethoven to bop. The acoustics are excellent. As a matter of fact, you can hear a pin drop from the highest seat."

How perfect in the birthplace of democracy that the cheapest seats have the best sound!

Natural woods at the base of the Acropolis surround the picturesque Temple of Hephaestus. The meadow is full of the same yellow wildflowers as on Hydra. My heart flies back there.

At 5pm, Sotiris leaves me to attend a grand-daughter's birthday celebration. What a generous way to spend his afternoon—sharing his city with a total stranger.

A Piece of My Heart

By this time, I've tried the numbers ten times.

I wander down to the Monastiraki flea-market again, dodging the t-shirts and caps until I reach the antiques. Inside tiny shops, furniture is packed so tightly there's hardly space to move, making it a challenge to navigate between the treasures.

In Ghikas' time, Hydra's shipowners were renowned for bringing back the finest furniture from all over Europe—ornate pieces like the ones I'm seeing here, from gilded mirrors to *escritoires*.

A jewellery vendor called Giorgios offers me the deal of the century—400 euros for a piece marked 1200. Only for me. Only today. His fun is infectious, and we laugh.

But even his warm hug, cheerful despite making no sale, can't distract me. My mind is elsewhere.

Crossing Syntagma Square on my way home, I see a demonstration in front of the parliament. Normally a crowd in a foreign country would set me on edge, but there's a calmness about the gathering. Later, from the hotel rooftop, drink in hand, I watch as the attendees listen respectfully then march away together with music and banners. It's almost soothing.

I read a little of the book Sotiris gave me. Ghikas would have loved this: "Out of this minute island have come some of the greatest sailors that the Mediterranean has ever bred." And, at the start of the War of Independence in 1821, the Kountouriotis family was estimated to be worth £2,000,000 sterling. Imagine that! And I was intrigued to learn that another Hydriot commander, Saktouris, was "rather given to piracy." Seems Ghikas wasn't exactly the only one dabbling in that line of work.

But it's hard to focus on reading when my brain keeps circling back to those unanswered calls.

Tomorrow, I tell myself. Tomorrow someone will answer.

Before I go to sleep, with a delicious tiredness creeping over me, I sit quietly on the bed, phone in hand. My fingers hover over the screen.

I dial the first number.

It rings once, twice... Rings out. Nothing.

I sigh and try the second.

One ring. Two...

And then someone picks up.

18

ANTÍO ELLÁDA: FAREWELL HELLAS

"Kalispéra, Dimitris Mavrideros edó."
"Hello, is that Mister Mavrideros? This is Shelley Dark speaking."
A brief pause.
"Yes, Mrs. Dark, how may I assist you?"
A small sigh escapes me—this formal tone reminds me of Sotiris earlier today. There's a distinct courtesy here, almost ceremonious, with an expectation it will be returned. At home, we expect manners too, but the Australian approach is much more relaxed.

"I've been in Ýdra doing research for a novel about a Hydriot who ended up a convict in Australia, Mister Mavrideros, and I'm flying back to Australia tomorrow. If you have time, I would love to meet you before I go."

Note my pronunciation of EE-druh!

"I'm sorry, Mrs. Dark, but I have the 'flu at the moment. I cannot see anyone."

Oh no! No! So close!

"I'm sorry to hear that. I hope you feel better soon." I explain that I'm tracing a young man who lived during the War of Independence.

For a second, the line crackles with silence.

Have I lost him?

But then his voice comes back, brighter, livelier than before. "Perfect, Mrs Dark. I will most certainly be able to help you. Ydra and the Greek Revolution are my exact areas of genealogical specialty. You have come to the right place."

Relief floods through me so fast that I nearly miss his next words. "Send me a letter detailing exactly what you want, and I'll be happy to assist."

This is it! I press a hand to my chest, pulse racing as I take a deep breath. "I... I can't thank you enough, Mister Mavrideros. The man's surname was Voulgaris."

"What a coincidence, Mrs Dark. I'm writing a book about the family."

The big breakthrough! I'm dancing inside.

Stay calm, Shell.

I squeak out, 'May I have your email address, please, Mister Mavrideros?' My pencil is poised, but I'm squeezing it hard enough to break it.

"Oh, Mrs Dark," he says. "I am an old-fashioned man. I'm afraid I use only the post."

Post? Who uses post? I nearly snap the pencil.

I take a deep breath. A slight setback, that's all.

He gives me his residential address, and I feel a spark of excitement bubbling back up. "Thank you for your time, Mr. Mavrideros. I'll make sure the letter is posted before I leave."

"It's my pleasure, Mrs. Dark. Safe travels back to Australia!"

His warmth matches my relief. This is happening. I'm grinning.

Before I go to sleep, I draft the letter and email it to Mina, the butler. But after the excitement, I barely sleep.

NOW I'M awake on our last day in Greece.

There's an email from Mina, saying she'll print the letter for me to sign, stamp it, and post it herself. She must be wondering how I've survived this long without adult supervision.

After breakfast, I head to the 6th-floor reception, thank her for her saintly efficiency and sign the letter with all the gravitas of a statesman brokering a world peace treaty.

Ok. Done. I feel lighter already.

But with only a few hours left in Athens, it's pressure-cooker time to squeeze every last drop out of every minute. I've signed up to write this novel, and suddenly, I'm aware of how much more I need to know. What did Ghikas actually wear? What did his father's house look like from the inside? My mind's buzzing with everything I still want to uncover.

City Hall, as Mrs. Adamopoulou suggested, can wait—no way am I diving into a red-tape swamp today. Maybe next time. Today, it's the Benaki Museum, and this time, I'll pay proper attention to the weapons and costumes.

Let's go buddies! We can watch the goose-stepping guards at the Parliament building, first, then take a quick stroll through the National Garden, and then the Benaki at opening time. That's where I'll find what I really need—the details that will help me breathe life into Ghikas' world.

But security in front of the parliament seems heightened, and troops are lined up in formation.

"Get out, get out! Back there! GET OUT!" It's an officer shouting, pointing wildly at us as if we've committed a capital offence.

He frantically herds us back to the intersection, while his fellow officer at the other end casually waves pedestrians towards us. I've walked straight into a Monty Python skit—the Minister for Silly Walks is still barking orders while tourists on the other side stroll through the middle of his military standoff. The whole thing is bizarre.

I learn later that a foreign diplomat is visiting.

I'm still laughing as I skip the changing of the guard and make my way to the National Garden, once Queen Amalia's back yard. She married King Otto in 1836—they were both Bavarian (huh?)—and she became the first queen of the new Greek monarchy.

I feel a kinship with her; after all, we both love a garden. She devoted three hours a day to hers and planted an entire avenue of Washingtonia palms. She'd be amazed to see these towering giants today, over twenty-five metres tall.

When I arrive at the Benaki Museum, a small queue has already formed. Behind the counter, a young woman wrestles with the ticket machine in what looks like a losing battle, her face a portrait of pure panic.

She scoots back on her roller chair and dives under the desk, reappearing moments later with her hands gripping the counter like she's clinging to a lifeboat. She glares at the machine, then grabs a fistful of her hair as if she wants to yank it out. A colleague swoops in, equally alarmed, and together they study the offending device like it's a bomb

Antío Elláda: Farewell Hellas

about to go off. The younger one, clearly the braver of the two, raises a cautious hand and delivers a light slap to its side—the kind of slap that suggests the machine might slap back. I stifle a laugh. They look up, red-faced, embarrassed.

"Please, come back later," the younger one says, waving us into the museum as if this is part of the entry plan.

I have a sneaking suspicion they're about to bring out the sledgehammer.

I head straight to the floor reserved for the Greek War of Independence. It's not another historical display; it's a gateway to Ghikas' world, with paintings and clothes, and furniture and weapons. I'm convinced he lived in this opulence as the son of a shipowner.

I linger at a display about Lord Byron. Looking gorgeous.

A life-sized representation of a Hydriot sailor clad in the traditional fez and vraka shows me the man I've been chasing. I stop at a painting of a ship visiting Hydra—I see him on board, musket slung over his shoulder, sword pushed into his waistband, ready to fight.

Photography allowed, I snap away.

This section of the museum uses oak and gilt carvings from Uncle Giorgios' old seraglio (the Turkish-style house built in 1802, but sadly, demolished in 1912) to recreate a room.

I know now that the Ottoman *seraglio* emphasises opulence and grandeur, reflecting power, while the typical Hydriot *archontikó* conceals any sign of wealth behind an austere facade. A reflection of the distinct personalities of the two regions.

So Uncle Giorgios' mansion was fancier with a wooden

upper floor that jutted out over the stone floors below, supported by visible wooden beams.

The interior, however, would have been much like Ghikas' own family mansion or any of the shipowners' homes on Hydra, which, while outwardly unassuming, concealed lavish interiors.

Grand marble entries could easily accommodate a welcoming party, and fragrant, flower-lined courtyards with trickling fountains set the stage for leisurely hookah sessions among friends. Each room had a designated purpose—from vibrant drawing rooms for animated discussions to grand halls ready for elaborate festivities and tucked-away nooks perfect for sharing secrets.

Men and women had their own sleeping areas, in keeping with Ottoman tradition.

It's easy to imagine Ghikas navigating these rooms, completely at ease in the familiar luxury hidden behind imposing stone walls.

In the Hydriot costume display, there's even an actual dress belonging to the wife of cousin Dimitris Voulgaris. Maria's great-great-great-grandmother.

But I'm pulled towards the wall where a painting of a Greek child of the era stares at me.

The Greek Boy. I see Ghikas.

Perhaps eight or ten, he has shoulder-length shining dark curls under a red fez with a black tassel. His serious, almost sad expression doesn't quite match his extravagant outfit—or maybe it's a sign of the battle it took to get him into it. He wears the white *fustanella* of the mainland, while Ghikas likely wore the more practical black *vraka* of the islands. His flowing white undershirt falls beneath a gold-

Antío Ellása: Farewell Hellas

embroidered red silk jacket, fastened with perfectly aligned buttons. Winged sleeves match the cummerbund, and gold thread adds a subtle brilliance. Even his soft shoes, laced up the legs, are red and gold, with matching embroidery—every detail's been carefully curated.

I remember Henry Post's comments about how well-dressed the Hydriots were. Intriguingly, I've since read that although Uncle George arrived on the island as governor wearing diamond-studded furs, with an extensive retinue and a Turkish secretary, he later forbade ostentatious clothing on Hydra.

I wonder if Ghikas ever looked like this, dressed up to the nines, unaware that life would take him far from his affluent beginnings to a convict's life in Australia.

I move on to the mosaics, especially the Byzantine. How is it that mosaic pieces stuck down in Roman times are still adhering to the floor beneath, thousands of years later? Will today's mosaic tiling, with all our space-age technology, stay glued down as long?

After hours of wandering, I finally return to pay my entrance fee. The young woman at the counter blinks at me in surprise, clearly wondering why I'd roam around for free all this time only to come back and pay.

For lunch, my last meal in Greece, I return to the hotel, where the rooftop restaurant overlooks the Acropolis. Five scallops grilled golden brown with superb kimchi, pureed potatoes, crunchy onions, fresh apple sticks, and bacon. It's a culinary masterpiece, the perfect farewell. I eat slowly, enjoying every mouthful.

I take in the view one last time. As the Acropolis glows in the afternoon sun, my thoughts drift to the letter to Mr.

Mavrideros. Hydra gave me much, but I'm still chasing answers—but maybe this new lead will be the breakthrough I need.

As I lay my napkin on the table, an Instagram notification pops up. An Insta-friend who's proficient in Greek offers to translate the Papamanolis book.

Maybe the tense won't be a problem for her. Maybe it will.

NOW AS I sit at the airport café waiting for my late afternoon flight, sipping my last Greek coffee, the smell of honeyed pastry mingles with the strange saltiness of a sea breeze that seems to have followed me from Hydra—probably a sign I'm losing my marbles. A small child runs past, her laughter echoing as her parents chase her, coats flapping. Life doesn't slow down; only old people do.

The calm and unhurried pace of those two weeks on Hydra has been pure bliss. Worthy of bottling as a tonic for modern life.

I understand now what Klein means about finding balance in aging. His "authentic old age" isn't about giving up or stopping completely; it's about adjusting the pace.

I knew his book wouldn't convince me to sit on a park bench feeding pigeons or swap my sneakers for a walking stick. But that wasn't his goal, and it's not mine either. Klein has encouraged me to find calm in the chaos, to live life a little more *andante*. And I've discovered a new obsession: Ghikas and writing about him—both as vital to me now as gardening once was.

I'll still order a dash of adrenalin to my authenticity—I

will remain one of his "forever youngs". But he's encouraged me to find joy in each moment—and I will—until I race off to the next one.

And I totally get Bertrand Russell's point in *In Praise of Idleness*—as Klein quoted him—about turning our free time into play—writing, after all, is about the sheer, ridiculous fun of making things up and calling it work.

OUR NEXT PROJECT, buddies—yes, I'm already planning it—will dive deeper into Ghikas' story in Australia, along with studying the craft of writing and more travel.

After that, how about a trip to Malta?

I'm dying to read the actual records of Ghikas and company's trial in Malta in 1828. Imagine the drama!

Then, after that, we could head to England and visit Kew Archives to handle the logbooks from the English ships: the anti-pirate vessel that captured them, the ship from Malta to England, and the one that took them to Australia.

We might even find correspondence about Hydra between the English captains who sailed these waters. And let's not forget County Cork, to see where Mary lived.

These past two weeks have lit a fire in me. I want to see the primary sources, touch the real history.

I'll need your company again.

Will you come with me?

My gate number is flashing. I gather my bags. Had you told me a couple of weeks ago that I'd leave here without a clear answer about Ghikas, it might have depressed me. But if I'm meant to find out, I will. And if not, I'll write my own ending. And if I drop dead halfway through writing this novel about Ghikas, or go ga-ga?

Does that mean I should have recognised my limitations and never started?

Of course not.

Whether my words end up on a best-seller list, in a "meh" pile, or gathering dust in a drawer, it doesn't matter. They're the side-effects of the adventure.

But the best part of being a writer? You can write anything, anywhere, at any age—jot ideas on a napkin in a café, draft chapters on a laptop mid-flight, balance an iPad and a cat on your lap while you're watching TV, or even tap away on your phone in your geriatric jammies with a hot chocolate on your bedside.

I think of John as I join the queue. Just as Klein finds comfort in his wife's presence at the end of his book, I'm glad that my partner-in-crime for the past 50 years is waiting for me at home.

Either of us could "shuffle off this mortal coil" at any time, as Shakespeare delicately put it—though John, ever the gentleman, would likely insist I go first. I'd better write my own glowing eulogy while I'm at it.

And if chasing our passions means we go sooner, so be it—better to burn out than fade away. Caring for each other will always come first, closely followed by endless lunches with family and friends, and stories told and retold over wine glasses that never run dry—while my digestion can stand it.

Thank you for coming along on this trip, buddies—your company, even virtual, has made it much more enjoyable for

Antío Elláda: Farewell Hellas

me—knowing I was writing for you. You've been my audience without giving me stage fright.

So yes, the jury is still out on whether I'm married to the descendant of a pirate, a freedom fighter, or a silly boy. It's a tough call because John shows signs of all three... And history, like my husband, isn't easily categorised with neat labels.

Except for Hydra. That one's easy: unforgettable.

I hand my boarding pass to the hostess, who greets me with a bright smile. As I step onto the plane—I know exactly what I want to do with the rest of my life.

Write, purely for the joy of it.

So buddies, until our next adventure together, *tha se periméno.*

I wait you.

A REQUEST

If *Hydra in Winter* brought you a smile, a chuckle, or even the urge to grab your passport, I'd be very happy if you'd leave an online review—they make a huge difference to a book's success.

You can do it on Amazon, Goodreads, or wherever you bought the book—just search for *Hydra in Winter by Shelley Dark*.

Want to stay in touch?

Join my readers' group at https://www.shelleydark.com/

Or drop me an email to shelleydarkwriter@gmail.com—I'd love to hear what you think!

So not only do I wait you, buddy. I wait your review!

www.ingramcontent.com/pod-product-compliance
Lightning Source LLC
Chambersburg PA
CBHW060607080526
44585CB00013B/719